Deterrence During Disarmament:
Deep Nuclear Reductions and International Security

James M. Acton

IISS The International Institute for Strategic Studies

The International Institute for Strategic Studies

Arundel House | 13–15 Arundel Street | Temple Place | London | WC2R 3DX | UK

First published March 2011 by **Routledge**
4 Park Square, Milton Park, Abingdon, Oxon, OX14 4RN

for **The International Institute for Strategic Studies**
Arundel House, 13–15 Arundel Street, Temple Place, London, WC2R 3DX, UK
www.iiss.org

Simultaneously published in the USA and Canada by **Routledge**
270 Madison Ave., New York, NY 10016

Routledge is an imprint of Taylor & Francis, an Informa Business

© 2011 The International Institute for Strategic Studies

DIRECTOR-GENERAL AND CHIEF EXECUTIVE John Chipman
EDITOR Nicholas Redman
ASSISTANT EDITOR Janis Lee
EDITORIAL Jeffrey Mazo, Sarah Johnstone, Ayse Abdullah
COVER/PRODUCTION John Buck
COVER IMAGES iStockphoto.com

The International Institute for Strategic Studies is an independent centre for research, information and debate on the problems of conflict, however caused, that have, or potentially have, an important military content. The Council and Staff of the Institute are international and its membership is drawn from almost 100 countries. The Institute is independent and it alone decides what activities to conduct. It owes no allegiance to any government, any group of governments or any political or other organisation. The IISS stresses rigorous research with a forward-looking policy orientation and places particular emphasis on bringing new perspectives to the strategic debate.

The Institute's publications are designed to meet the needs of a wider audience than its own membership and are available on subscription, by mail order and in good bookshops. Further details at www.iiss.org.

Printed and bound in Great Britain by Bell & Bain Ltd, Thornliebank, Glasgow

British Library Cataloguing in Publication Data
A catalogue record for this book is available from the British Library

Library of Congress Cataloging in Publication Data

ADELPHI series
ISSN 0567-932X

ADELPHI 417
ISBN 978-0-415-68182-7

Contents

ACKNOWLEDGEMENTS

This work was made possible through the generous support of the Strategic Programme Fund of the UK Foreign and Commonwealth Office, the Stanton Foundation and the William and Flora Hewlett Foundation. For research assistance, I would like to thank Marcy Fowler, Nima Gerami, Ellie Immerman, Kim Misher and Brian Radzinsky. I am also grateful to Jocelyn Soly for her creative insights and advice. For stimulating conversations on this subject and/or helpful comments on the manuscript, I would like to thank Elbridge Colby, Mark Fitzpatrick, Charles Glaser, Ed Ifft, Jeffrey Lewis, Brad Roberts, Scott Sagan, Paul Schulte, Heather Williams and, especially, Linton Brooks, Michael Gerson and George Perkovich. Of course, the contents of this study are my own responsibility.

To understand concerns about deep reductions, I conducted interviews with analysts and present and former officials from Russia, the United States and US allies as part of my research for this book. To ensure a frank discussion all interviews were conducted with a guarantee of anonymity. I have generally avoided referencing such interviews and instead point to identical arguments made in the open literature. However, I thank all those who agreed to be interviewed for being so generous with their time.

INTRODUCTION

The prospects for deep cuts in the American and Russian nuclear arsenals, while not yet propitious, are better than at any time since those arsenals were first built up. On 5 April 2009, in a major policy address in Prague, President Barack Obama recommitted the United States to seeking 'the peace and security of a world without nuclear weapons'.[1] Four days earlier, in a less noted but nonetheless highly significant development, his Russian counterpart Dmitry Medvedev had reaffirmed Russia's commitment to that same goal in a joint statement with Obama. The two leaders also outlined their vision for the disarmament process. They made it clear that they will work to reduce nuclear weapon stockpiles incrementally – first bilaterally and then multilaterally – in a 'step-by-step process'.[2] They also recognised that the complete elimination of nuclear weapons would be contingent on creating the necessary political and security conditions. These conditions would include the ability to effectively verify and enforce an abolition agreement and a new security architecture that would allow today's nuclear-armed states to protect their vital interests without nuclear weapons.[3]

Obama and Medvedev's first step was the New Strategic Arms Reduction Treaty (New START). This treaty, which provides for modest, verified reductions in deployed strategic weapons, was signed on 8 April 2010. The US Senate provided its advice and consent to ratification on 22 December 2010 by 71 votes to 26. In January 2011, Russia followed the US lead and completed its own ratification process. The two states are now starting to focus their attention on a more ambitious successor.

The disarmament 'glide path' on which Russia and the US have embarked naturally raises questions about how further reductions would affect international security: do these former Cold War adversaries have bloated arsenals that could, over time, be cut significantly without any negative impact on security? Or are significant improvements in the security environment a prerequisite for further reductions of any significance? These concerns were not really raised by New START because the reductions it mandates are so modest. However, New START's opponents – and even some of its proponents – have expressed their misgivings about the effect of deeper reductions.[4] A debate about 'how much is enough' cannot be put off indefinitely; indeed, within the American and Russian security communities, it is already being joined.[5] Most significantly, the Obama administration's own Nuclear Posture Review, while broadly endorsing the goal of deeper reductions, flags up various potential concerns about their consequences for international security and pledges to examine them further.[6]

The issue of deep reductions must, almost inevitably, be examined from the perspective of the two most heavily armed nuclear powers, since they are of primary importance in steering the debate.[7] Underlying much of the concern in Russia and the United States is the assumption that possessing large nuclear arsenals is the norm and therefore that deterrence at low numbers would be a step into the unknown. Yet, in building huge arsenals during the Cold War, the USSR and the United States did not exhibit 'normal nuclear behaviour'.[8] Of the ten states that built nuclear weapons indigenously, only they built arsenals containing more than a few hundred redundant warheads.[9] The eight 'nuclear minnows' do not seem to have been less effective than the superpowers in deterring aggression. Moreover, given that they were not engaged in an arms race, as the US and USSR were, their deterrence relations actually appear to have been more stable. This observation suggests that deterrence at low numbers may not be as unprecedented or as difficult as is sometimes perceived in Russia and the US.

Of course, unlike other nuclear-armed states today, the US has foreign security commitments (as did the Soviet Union). Perhaps the most important experience for assessing the effect of deep reductions is, therefore, crises that resulted from those commitments early in the Cold War when one or both of the superpowers had only small arsenals. This experience provides empirical evidence that can be used to test the validity of theoretical arguments about deterrence at low numbers. The principal conclusion drawn from this evidence is that most, but not all, of the problems and instabilities often associated with low numbers of warheads are either not related to arsenal size or are only weakly affected by it. A range of other factors – including credibility, doctrine and survivability – are more important in effecting instability or deterrence failures. To the extent that these are problematic, larger arsenals do little or nothing to solve them.

Why is there renewed interest in nuclear arms reductions?

The intellectual foundations of the Obama administration's nuclear-weapons policy are radically different from those of its predecessor and have led to a renewed interest in arms reductions. Before exploring these differences, however, it is important to recognise that, in terms of the actual actions taken by the two administrations, there has been a greater degree of continuity than is generally realised. In its Nuclear Posture Review, the Obama administration modestly reduced the role of nuclear weapons in US national security strategy and identified strengthening conventional deterrence as a way of marginalising them further.[10] The George W. Bush administration also sought, on balance, to reduce the role of nuclear weapons and, by developing new roles for conventional weapons, took modest steps in that direction (although it managed to give the opposite impression).[11] Both administrations sought to modernise the nuclear enterprise, albeit in different ways. (The Bush administration tried, unsuccessfully, to secure funding to build new warheads, whereas the Obama administration has been more successful in seeking funding to renew the nuclear-weapons production infrastructure.) Shortly after entering office, both administrations negotiated a modest arms-control treaty with Russia. There are, of course, some important differences between the two treaties. The 2002 Moscow Treaty limits only deployed strategic warheads (to between 1,700 and 2,200). Unlike New START, it does not limit launchers or delivery systems and does not contain a verification regime. However, New START does follow the precedent set by the Moscow Treaty of constraining the overall size of American or Russian nuclear forces without placing any restrictions on their structure.

None of this is to deny the important policy differences between the two administrations – their differing views on the Comprehensive Test Ban Treaty (CTBT) being a particularly stark example.[12] However, what this demonstrates is that the biggest difference has been in their objectives rather than their actions. Most strikingly, President Obama has spearheaded an approach that embraces the goal of a world without nuclear weapons. Any realistic pathway to this goal would involve passing through a regime of low numbers.

The reasons for the renewed American interest in nuclear disarmament are often misunderstood. Administration officials have stated that progress towards disarmament by the nuclear-weapon states is a necessary step in promoting non-proliferation. Yet, they have not always been clear about how they perceive the linkage between disarmament and non-proliferation and consequently they have allowed their position to be seriously misrepresented. Critics of the administration charge it with naïvety for expecting Iran or North Korea to rethink their nuclear ambitions in light of disarmament steps by the US.[13] In fact, the administration expects no such thing. It is not hoping to influence the behaviour of Iran or North Korea directly, but rather to garner the support of other non-nuclear-weapon states (the vast majority of which are in full compliance with their obligations under the Non-Proliferation Treaty, or NPT) in strengthening the non-proliferation regime.[14]

Most of the steps that the US considers critical to non-proliferation – tougher sanctions against states that break the rules, strengthened safeguards and enhanced export controls – require the active support of non-nuclear-weapon states. However, many of these states refuse to take such steps, citing as their justification the failure of the nuclear-weapon states to work towards their NPT commitment to disarm. There are reasons to suppose that, at least in some cases, this explanation is an honest justification rather than a convenient excuse. Key non-nuclear-weapon states – including Argentina, Brazil, South Africa and Turkey – while not welcoming proliferation, do not regard it to be as much of a threat as the US and other

Western states do. However, they do vigorously object to the two-tier nature of the current non-proliferation regime with its division between nuclear-weapon states and non-nuclear-weapon states. They argue that without good faith efforts by the nuclear-weapon states to work towards the complete elimination of nuclear weapons, as required by article VI of the NPT, this 'discrimination' would be 'intolerable'.[15] It would, therefore, be perfectly logical for such states to condition their support for tougher non-proliferation measures on progress towards disarmament. And, it is these states – not Iran or North Korea – that the Obama administration hopes to influence by taking steps towards disarmament. How successful this strategy is likely to be in practice is hard to predict; at the time of writing, less than two years since the president's Prague speech, it is probably too early to judge.[16]

The role of arms control in US–Russia relations marks a second, profound intellectual disagreement between the Bush and Obama administrations. The Bush administration saw arms control as a legacy of the Cold War that actually undermined US–Russia relations. It rejected 'the adversarial arms control negotiations of the Soviet era – where teams of lawyers drafted hundreds of pages of treaty text, and each side worked to gain the upper hand, while focusing on ways to preserve a balance of nuclear terror'.[17] Bush administration officials argued then – and still argue now – that

> if we want a normal relationship with Russia, we need to move beyond Cold-War approaches. We need to base our relations on common interests and joint efforts to deal with today's security challenges, such as countering nuclear terrorism and managing the expansion of nuclear energy... .[18]

In contrast, the Obama administration views traditional arms control as a 'cornerstone' of its efforts to reset relations with Russia.[19] Whatever the intellectual merits of the Bush administration's arguments about creating a 'normal' US–Russian relationship, the political reality is that Russia does not appear to want Washington's version of normality. Its large nuclear arsenal is (along with its permanent seat on the United Nations Security Council) the last vestige of its superpower status and it therefore places considerable value on the special status derived from being a participant in high-profile bilateral nuclear-arms-control negotiations. Konstantin Kosachev, State Duma International Affairs Committee Chairman, captured the mood of the Russian establishment in January 2011 when he stated: 'Russia is once again perceived as an equal partner with whom you can and should negotiate.'[20] In private, Obama administration officials have argued that by increasing the value the US-Russia relationship to Moscow – including by entering into arms-control negotiations – they can enhance the prospects for Russian cooperation on issues that are important to Washington. The apparent success of President Obama's 'reset' of relations with Moscow, which has yielded increased Russian assistance in areas critical to US national security, including Iran and Afghanistan, certainly lends credence to these claims.

What is less clear, however, is whether further arms-control negotiations with Russia will further improve the US–Russian relationship – and, for that matter, whether the Obama administration expects them to. Moscow is likely to enjoy the prestige associated with being a participant in further negotiations. However, future negotiations will have to tackle a set of highly contentious issues, such as tactical nuclear weapons, ballistic-missile defence and high-precision conventional weapons, which did not have be settled (or, in the case of tactical nuclear weapons, even discussed) in New START because its reductions were so modest (because of New START's counting rules the actual reduction in US and Russia deployed strategic warheads could end up being less than 10% below their 2010 levels). These issues, which are considered at greater length below, have the potential to effect an acrimonious and unproductive series of negotiations. That said, failing to engage Russia on further arms control would not result in any of these issues simply disappearing. They are irritants to the bilateral relationship and if not addressed they have the potential to undermine it. On balance, therefore, the potential benefits to US–Russia relations of further arms-control negotiations appear to outweigh the risks. Of course, talks will have to be planned and structured carefully to maximise the prospects for success.

So far, this discussion has focused on Washington's motivation for pursuing deep reductions. This reflects the reality that the US is considerably more interested in nuclear disarmament than Russia. Medvedev may have explicitly endorsed working towards a world without nuclear weapons, to the surprise of many observers, but much of the military and political establishment in Moscow remains deeply sceptical of that goal.[21] As discussed below, some of their concerns are strategic and could be eased by arms-control measures that address Moscow's concerns about America's conventional superiority. Indeed, in a positive development, a number of highly respected former Russian military officers and officials have started to sketch out the conditions that would be required for Russia to make deep reductions in its arsenal.[22] However, as noted above, Moscow also appears to believe that it derives considerable status from its possession of a large nuclear arsenal. This status, which makes negotiations with the US attractive, reduces the appeal of actual reductions.

Assessing the effect of deep reductions: deterrence effectiveness and strategic stability

The role of nuclear weapons is usually cast in terms of 'deterrence by punishment', that is, threatening to inflict damage on an adversary in response to specified actions to try to convince it that the costs of aggression would outweigh the benefits. In arguments for the retention of large arsenals, a second possible role is often advocated for nuclear weapons: 'deterrence by denial', that is, deterrence by the threat to prevent an adversary from achieving its desired objectives. In either case, deterrence can be aimed at preserving a state's own vital interests (this is known as central deterrence) or those of its allies (extended deterrence). Given that nuclear deterrence still plays an important role in the defence doctrines of both Russia and the United States, it is important to consider whether deep reductions would undermine the effectiveness of deterrence.[23]

Strategic stability is a more esoteric concept. It has two components: crisis stability and armament stability (for reasons explained below, the term 'armament stability' is preferred here to the more usual 'arms race stability'). Each of these concepts requires more explanation.

Deterrence involves a potential aggressor comparing the consequences of action and inaction. Intuitively, we tend to think that inaction would simply maintain the status quo and hence be cost free. Yet, in some scenarios, failing to act can carry significant risks. Specifically, if there is a significant advantage to striking first and a state believes, rightly or wrongly, that its adversary might be planning to do so, the costs of inaction could be high, generating an incentive to act quickly and land the first blow. Deterrence is said to be unstable if, in a crisis, the fear of being pre-empted creates pressure to pre-empt.

In a famous 1958 essay, Thomas Schelling, who is principally responsible for developing the theory of crisis stability, illustrated his point with an example that – although not quite an everyday happening – must have occurred many times in states with liberal gun laws:

> If I go downstairs to investigate a noise at night, with a gun in my hand, and find myself face to face with a burglar who has a gun in his hand, there is a danger of an outcome that neither of us desires. Even if he prefers just to leave quietly, and I wish him to, there is a danger that he may think I want to shoot, and shoot first. Worse, there is danger that he may think that I think he wants to shoot. Or he may think that I think he thinks I want to shoot. And so on.[24]

During the Cold War, the possibility that nuclear weapons might generate crisis dynamics similar to hand guns proved a persistent worry. Specifically, there was a fear that, in a crisis, one of the superpowers might come to believe that the other was planning a nuclear attack and thus strike first in an attempt to destroy as much of its adversary's nuclear force as possible and limit the damage it would suffer. The result would be a nuclear war that neither side desired. In fact, as discussed in Chapter three, there are other reasons besides the desire to limit damage why a state that fears it is about to be the victim of nuclear weapons might use them first. However, whatever the specific 'mechanism' of instability, highly survivable nuclear forces that cannot be destroyed in a pre-emptive first strike are the key to ensuring crisis stability. Indeed, the principal intellectual justification for arms control – at least in the United States – was to enhance crisis stability by forcing each side to adopt a nuclear posture that reduced the advantages of striking first. A key US goal of the Cold War arms-control process was the elimination of intercontinental ballistic missiles (ICBMs) capable of carrying multiple independent re-entry vehicles (MIRVs). These weapons undermine crisis stability because, in general, targeting them would destroy more warheads than were used in the attack. This creates an incentive to attack them early in a crisis and therefore an incentive for the possessor to use them quickly.

The second component of strategic stability is armament stability (more usually termed arms race stability). Armament stability is said to be high when no state has an incentive to build up its nuclear arsenal. In theory, armament stability and crisis stability are closely connected.[25] If crisis stability is low because a state is worried about the survivability of its forces then it might respond by building more. If doing so compromises the survivability of an opponent's forces, the opponent might also build up. This, however, could exacerbate the concerns of the first state, resulting in an arms race.

In practice, however, the reasons why states build up their arsenals are much more complicated than simple concerns about survivability. As discussed further in Chapter four, the American and Soviet build-ups during the Cold War were motivated much more by domestic politics, bureaucratic politics and doctrine than by any calculation of how many weapons would survive a first strike. To complicate matters further, states can also refrain from building up their arsenals, in spite of concerns about survivability. During the Cold War, for instance, China chose not to engage in the arms race even though its small nuclear force really was compromised by the much larger size of the superpowers' arsenals. Since a build-up by one state does not always trigger an adversary to do likewise, it may be more illuminating for current purposes to discard the usual term 'arms race stability' in favour of 'armament stability', or in assessing the incentives to rearm after reductions, 'rearmament stability'.

The relevance of strategic stability in assessing force posture has always been the subject of debate. Some analysts see it as an enduringly important concept. There is a long-standing concern that deep reductions would reduce the survivability of Russia's already vulnerable nuclear forces and thus undermine both crisis and armament stability. Historian Lawrence Freedman, for example, argues that instability might arise at low numbers as a result of 'more delicate nuclear balances when small numbers multiply the impact of any aggressive first strike'.[26] Although less explicit, the 2010 Nuclear Posture Review appears to indicate that the Obama administration has similar concerns in its identification of 'strategic stability' as a metric for assessing the desirability of further reductions.[27]

However, since the end of the Cold War the broad consensus around the importance of strategic stability has been eroding, at least in the United States and amongst its allies. (In an interesting turn of events, Russia, which remained sceptical of the concept throughout much of the Cold War, has now become its strongest proponent.) Those who reject the concept of strategic stability have three broad grounds for doing so.

Firstly, some argue that strategic stability has become irrelevant because the Cold War ended any prospect of nuclear war. In 2002, during the Senate hearings about the Moscow Treaty, for example, then US Secretary of State Colin Powell argued that that there was 'a new strategic relationship' between Russia and the US, that there was 'nothing to go to war about', and that concepts of strategic stability were therefore 'outdated'.[28] This argument is disingenuous. Recognising that the end of Cold War had significantly reduced the chance of a conflict between Russia and the US, the Bush administration ceased to treat Russia as an 'immediate contingency' in its nuclear planning.[29] However, it continued to plan for the use of nuclear weapons against Russia in scenarios that it regarded as 'plausible', if unlikely.[30] In large part because of the United States' security commitments to NATO, the 2001 Nuclear Posture Review (or at least, it is claimed, leaked fragments of it) stated that 'Russia faces many strategic problems around its periphery and its future course cannot be charted with certainty. U.S. planning must take this into account.'[31] Should relations with Russia deteriorate to the point where the use of these contingency plans were conceivable, it would manifestly be in the interests of the United States that Russia did not feel pressured into using nuclear weapons if Moscow believed (almost certainly incorrectly) that Washington was considering using them first.

Secondly, some analysts argue that, by focusing on the nuclear balance, the concept of strategic stability provides a distorted picture of international relations. They argue that the stability of relations between states depends much more upon factors such as values, interests, ideologies, economics and conventional forces than upon nuclear forces.[32] They stress that the huge geopolitical changes that have taken place since the end of the Cold War – including the easing of international tensions and increased economic interdependence – have further marginalised the concept of strategic stability.

This criticism is correct, but irrelevant. Most of those who argue that strategic stability remains an important concept do not regard it as the key factor in determining the nature of international relations but, more modestly, as an important metric for assessing nuclear force posture. Hopefully, because of all the changes that have occurred since the end of the Cold War, international relations will never again be stretched to the point where the use of a nuclear weapon is conceivable. But, nuclear-armed states worry that they could and therefore retain their nuclear arsenals. If there is a serious crisis in which the use of nuclear weapons is contemplated, it is manifestly in everyone's interests that none of the belligerents feels pressured to use nuclear weapons first out of the fear of being second. Admittedly, the term 'strategic stability' is sometimes used very vaguely as a sort of catch-all concept meaning 'international peace and security', and this encourages criticism of the kind rebutted here. However, the fact that the term is misused does not undermine the validity of the concept.

The third criticism of strategic stability comes from those who believe that the credibility of US nuclear threats could hang on the country's ability to significantly reduce the damage it would suffer in a nuclear war, especially in the case of threats made in the defence of an ally. Accordingly, they argue that, in some circumstances, the United States needs to be able to eliminate all or most of an opponent's nuclear forces (using a combination of nuclear and non-nuclear weapons and ballistic missile defences) in order to deter it.[33] They argue that the US should not take steps to assure potential adversaries of the survivability of their forces because doing so would undermine the effectiveness of deterrence (particularly extended deterrence). In response to worries about crisis stability they simply reject the notion that 'the primary motive for one country to attack another springs simply from a misunderstanding that the other side might attack.'[34] This critique of crisis stability is the most substantial and it cannot be rejected out of hand. For this reason, strategic stability is not an adequate criterion, by itself, for assessing force posture; deterrence effectiveness must be treated as an explicit metric for that purpose as well.

In mapping out American and Russian concerns, five principal objections to deep reductions arise. Deep cuts, it is argued, would

- undermine central deterrence and lead to more conflict;
- undermine extended deterrence and the security of US allies;
- exacerbate concerns about arsenal survivability and undermine crisis stability;

- quickly be reversed because rearmament stability would be low; and
- lead to the smaller arsenals of other nuclear-armed states increasing in relative importance and undermine strategic stability as a result of multipolarity.

Parameters and assumptions

'Deep reductions' are defined here as cuts in the US and Russian arsenals to 500 warheads of all types (deployed and non-deployed, strategic and tactical) on each side, with limits on other nuclear-armed states (as discussed below). This number, equal to the approximate maximum size of the British or French arsenals during the Cold War, was recently highlighted by the International Commission on Non-proliferation and Disarmament as a key milestone on the road to a world without nuclear weapons.[35]

To put reductions of this scale in context, it is helpful to note that the current Russian and US operational stockpiles number roughly 5,000 warheads each.[36] As shown in Table one, their total stockpiles (which include weapons awaiting dismantlement and, in the Russian case, weapons in reserve) are even larger and account for about 95% of the global total. Russian

Table 1: **The world's nuclear-weapon arsenals**[37]

State	Number of warheads
Russia	12,000*
United States	9,400
France	300
China	240*
United Kingdom	225
Pakistan	100*
Israel	70*
India	70*
DPRK	6*

All figures subject to significant uncertainties have been marked by a *. Sources: David Albright and Paul Brannan, 'The North Korean Plutonium Stock, February 2007', Institute for Science and International Security, 20 February 2007, p. 14; David E. Sanger and Eric Schmitt, 'Pakistani Nuclear Arms Pose Challenge to U.S. Policy', *New York Times*, 31 January 2011; and Robert S. Norris and Hans M. Kristensen, 'Global Nuclear Weapons Inventories, 1945– 2010', *Bulletin of the Atomic Scientists*, vol. 66, no. 4, July–August 2010, pp. 78.

and US arsenals last totalled fewer than 500 weapons in 1956 (when Russia was, of course, the Soviet Union) and 1950.[38] Russian and US nuclear forces are discussed in greater detail in the Appendix (p. 101).

The analysis of the effect of deep reductions on international security is built upon three main assumptions. Firstly, it is assumed that international relations (both between Russia and the US and with their potential adversaries) will not get significantly better or worse than they are today. This is not to postulate the absence of serious crises in which the use of nuclear weapons would be credible, but rather that there will not be a sustained and serious deterioration of international relations akin to a second Cold War. But there are undoubtedly areas where modest confidence-building would be helpful.

Secondly, it is assumed that deep reductions will not be unilateral. Treaty-mandated arms reductions will certainly remain bilateral for the time being. However, Russia and the United States have made it clear that if reductions are to continue, China, France and the UK must join a multilateral process before Russia and the US reach their level (and, in addition, no other nuclear-armed state must challenge Russia and the US numerically).[39] Regardless of whether a difficult multilateral process is strategically necessary, it will be required as a matter of political reality.

Thirdly, it is also assumed that Russia and the US will agree to limit both tactical warheads and non-deployed warheads, as made explicit in the definition of 500 warheads of all types. Today, only deployed strategic warheads are subject to arms control. In 2010, the United States had an estimated 2,000 such warheads and Russia about 2,600.[40] As discussed in the Appendix, Russia has a much larger number of tactical nuclear weapons than the US. This is a matter of concern to the US and its allies and the US has publicly insisted that Russian tactical nuclear weapons must be included in the reductions process.[41] It remains to be seen whether this proves possible; if it does not, then the US will not consent to deep reductions. Similarly, Russia is deeply concerned about the American advantage in non-deployed strategic warheads. If the US does not agree to limit non-deployed weapons then Russia will not agree to take part in the reductions process. It is further assumed that, in addition to warheads, launchers and delivery vehicles will be verifiably limited and destroyed – as in most past arms-control agreements.

It is obvious that, as a result of the need to include tactical and non-deployed weapons and to involve China, France and the UK, arms-control negotiations could become extremely complicated. As a result of these complexities, it is far from obvious that they would succeed. However, in order to analyse the fundamental question of whether we should even bother trying to significantly reduce the number of nuclear weapons in the world, it is assumed here that all these hurdles could be successfully overcome.

CHAPTER ONE

Central deterrence

Although Russia and the United States seek to deter direct aggression from various states, their most challenging task from a military planning perspective is still deterring one another. This is because each has the capability to destroy a significant fraction of the other's nuclear forces in a first strike. Russia and the US must, therefore, each assess whether the warheads that would survive a first strike are sufficient for deterrence. Twenty years after the end of the Cold War this may seem to be a rather extreme criterion. However, given that both states still worry that US security commitments to NATO could lead to direct conflict, it is what conservative military planning requires.

Unless the US and Russia were to eliminate all of their delivery systems except for silo-based ICBMs, it is virtually impossible to estimate with any confidence how many nuclear weapons would survive a first strike at low numbers, at least not without making unreasonable assumptions. For instance, in a much-noted 2006 article, US political scientists Keir A. Lieber and Daryl G. Press argued that an American first strike could, to a high degree of confidence, completely eliminate the Russian nuclear arsenal.[1] However, in doing so, they had to assume that the Russian nuclear force was at its lowest possible state of alert, that is, all ballistic-missile submarines (SSBNs) were in port and all nuclear-armed bombers and road-mobile ICBMs were in their shelters. Once a crisis began, however, Russia could start to disperse these forces and enhance their survivability. Thus, Leiber and Press's calculations were relevant only to a US first strike against Russia in peacetime or at the very start of a crisis (something that is virtually unimaginable). Once a crisis is under way and states have taken steps to disperse their nuclear forces, it becomes much harder to calculate how many warheads would survive a first strike.

Perhaps the best that can be said is that Russia's road-mobile ICBMs are, after dispersal, almost certainly the most survivable element of its nuclear forces. As discussed further below, at *least* 10–20% of these weapons would be likely to survive a first strike. It bears emphasising that this is probably an extremely conservative estimate and that a significantly higher percentage would probably survive. If, therefore, single-warhead road-mobile ICBMs were to make up a significant fraction of a Russian force of 500 warheads, then it should have tens of nuclear weapons, if not more, available for retaliation after a US first strike. The US force is more survivable than Russia's (in large part because of its SSBN force and its significant lead over Russia in anti-submarine warfare). It is probably safe to assume, therefore, that, at low numbers, more US weapons would survive a Russian first strike than Russian warheads would survive an American first strike. With fewer than 225 warheads, the United Kingdom is currently able to keep at least one SSBN loaded with 48 warheads at sea at any given time. If, therefore, the US were to prioritise its SSBN force then, with a total stockpile of 500 warheads, it should be able to keep at least 100 warheads continuously at sea. Ideally these would be based on, say, four SSBNs to reduce the impact of any one submarine being destroyed. In a crisis more SSBNs could be put to sea, temporarily increasing that number of highly survivable warheads to 150 or perhaps even 200.

The case for the efficacy of small arsenals

The sufficiency of small arsenals for central deterrence is often presented in terms of the huge damage that can be wrought by even a handful of nuclear weapons.[2] Those that make this argument recognise that the use of a small number of nuclear weapons would not necessarily result in immense damage. (The use of a few warheads against isolated troops, say, would not.) Rather, their argument is that in deciding whether to attack a nuclear-armed state, a potential adversary would have to consider what could happen.

The destructive power of a few nuclear weapons is not by itself, however, sufficient for effective deterrence. In theory, if political leaders performed careful calculations and 'discounted' the cost of a nuclear strike by its likelihood, arsenal size could matter greatly.[3] The effectiveness of small arsenals therefore hinges on a second condition that relates to the psychology of decision-makers facing nuclear threats. Two 'ideal models' of decision-making are shown schematically in Figure 1 (overleaf). Decision-maker 'A', who thinks like McGeorge Bundy, US national security adviser to Presidents John F. Kennedy and Lyndon B. Johnson, would regard a nuclear strike on one city as utterly catastrophic and would view the marginal cost of losing each extra city as being relatively small.[4] Decision-maker B, modelled on nuclear strategist Herman Kahn, would regard the loss of each extra city (up to a point) as being a significantly worse outcome.[5] Leaders who think like Bundy are likely to be deterred by small arsenals, even if the probability of nuclear retaliation is relatively small. In contrast, if the chance of nuclear war is slim, large arsenals might be needed to deter those who share Kahn's beliefs.

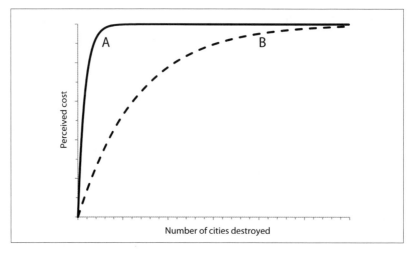

Figure 1: Two different decision-making models for leaders facing nuclear threats: Bundy (A) and Kahn (B). This graph is intended only as an aid for conceptual understanding. It is not quantitatively accurate.

The difference between these two ways of thinking was perfectly captured by Stanley Kubrick's 1964 film, *Dr. Strangelove or: How I Learned to Stop Worrying and Love the Bomb*. Believing that nuclear war is imminent, General 'Buck' Turgidson (a Kahn-like thinker) urges President Merkin Muffley (who exhibits a Bundy-like response) to strike first and radically improve the outcome of the war, or as he puts it, 'to make a choice ... between two admittedly regrettable, but nevertheless, distinguishable post-war environments: one where you got twenty million people killed, and the other where you got a hundred and fifty million people killed'. Muffley tells the general that he is talking about mass murder, not war.

Of course, fiction does not provide evidence about how past leaders have actually reasoned. For that it is necessary to turn to history. While it is impossible to discount the possibility that some future leaders will share Kahn's thinking, past leaders appear to have thought like Bundy. Soviet premier Nikita Khrushchev, for instance, reflected Bundy's view of nuclear war in a letter to President Kennedy on 26 October 1962, at the height of the Cuban Missile Crisis, where he talked of 'the catastrophe of thermonuclear war' and 'reciprocal extermination'. Admittedly, Khrushchev's comments can be interpreted in other ways – either reflecting the belief that limited nuclear war was impossible, or simply as brinkmanship – but his own actions are revealing. In 1958, he rejected plans for a large build-up of Soviet missile forces and instead settled for a 'second-best strategic posture' consisting of a small ICBM force.[6] 'Missiles are not cucumbers', he explained, 'one cannot eat them, and one does not require more than a certain number in order to ward off an attack.'[7] Khrushchev's subsequent reversal resulted from his belief that the United States thought it could exploit nuclear superiority; there is no evidence he changed his mind about the consequences of a few nuclear weapons on Soviet cities.

It bears emphasising that the argument that nuclear deterrence is not enhanced by larger numbers does not lead to the conclusion that it is always guaranteed to be successful. If the possibility of nuclear escalation is judged to be sufficiently incredible, it may be dismissed entirely. Argentina made this calculation about the British response when it invaded the Falkland Islands in 1982.[8] In these cases, a larger arsenal would not make a difference.

China provides an important example of the success of a small arsenal in effectively deterring powers that are superior both in terms of conventional and nuclear weapons, namely the US and the USSR.[9] Indeed, it is notable that China has never built up its arsenal significantly, even though it has long had the resources to do so.[10] Critics of the thesis that China's small arsenal has always proved an effective deterrent, including US political scientist Lyle J. Goldstein, point to the Sino-Soviet border crisis of 1969 and argue that, during this crisis, the Soviet Union seriously considered a first strike on China and that the possibility of Chinese nuclear retaliation played little, if any, role in deterring it.[11] In fact, even if this disputed interpretation is correct, it is not really an argument against small arsenals. As Goldstein's own analysis makes clear, the real problem was not that the Chinese arsenal was small; rather, it was its extreme vulnerability, exacerbated by what the Soviets believed was excellent intelligence on Beijing's nuclear arsenal, making them confident in their ability to execute a 'splendid' first strike. Moreover, key Soviet cities would not have been within range of any Chinese weapons that happened to escape a strike. A Chinese larger arsenal, per se, would not have solved any of these problems. A differently structured and protected arsenal may have done so.

It is also significant that the main causes of US–Soviet crises when one or both states had small arsenals did not include one protagonist having too few nuclear weapons to deter the other. Their primary cause was, of course, the political disputes underlying the Cold War. The belief that war was inevitable in the long run bolstered the case of preventive war advocates.[12] In addition, the vulnerability of the Soviet arsenal encouraged US planning for a first strike and stoked Russian fears of inferiority. This final problem may have been alleviated slightly by a larger Soviet arsenal. However, the real problem was the vulnerability of Soviet bombers (the only delivery vehicle the USSR could produce in large numbers until the mid-1960s). Fifty years on, it is notable those who question the thesis that nuclear weapons help prevent war between India and Pakistan do not argue that larger arsenals would reduce the likelihood of a deterrence failure.

The case for the deterrent value of small arsenals has been critiqued in numerous ways. The three critiques that are encountered most frequently today (including in interviews with American and Russian former officials and analysts) are mirror-imaging, countervalue targeting and tactical weapons.

Mirror imaging

One critique accuses proponents of small arsenals of mirror imaging – that is, incorrectly attributing their own values to others.[13] Specifically, some US analysts argue that potential US adversaries, including China, Iran, North Korea and Russia, may not value their populations and can only be deterred if the United States can hold at risk what they do value. Former US Deputy Assistant Secretary of Defence Keith B. Payne, for example, gives deeply buried bunkers as an example of what, to 'rogues and other potential [US] opponents' might consti- tute a key "value" target'.[14] He argues for a large and flexible enough US nuclear force to be able to 'threaten the wide array of targets potentially important for deterrence'. Indeed, it is important to realise that the US does not deliberately target civilians at the moment. Instead, its target list includes 'WMD infrastructure, military and national leadership and war- supporting infrastructure' on the grounds that these are what potential adversaries value the most.[15]

Russia is the most important case for assessing this argu- ment since, as noted above, no other state has anything like Russia's ability to attack US nuclear forces and hence reduce the number of available American warheads. (Moreover, it seems extremely unlikely that the United States would plan to use anything close to 500 nuclear weapons in any scenario involving Iran or North Korea, so deep reductions would prob- ably not affect US targeting plans at all in those cases.) One former senior official interviewed for this study argued that, to deter Russia effectively, the US might require the ability to effectively eliminate all its 'sources of state power': its nuclear and conventional military forces and its ability to utilise them (its military command and control system).[16] Many of the rele- vant targets in Russia are buried and can only be destroyed with nuclear weapons. Significant further cuts, it was argued, would undermine the United States' ability to perform this task.

The intellectual heritage of this argument is revealing. It stems directly from a similar argument advanced in the US during the late 1970s and 1980s, that US intelligence was mirror imaging its own belief in mutual deterrence onto the USSR and that the latter actually believed it could fight and win a nuclear war. Those who made this argument claimed the Soviet leadership believed that if it and its sources of power survived, the USSR could successfully recover from the huge civilian losses incurred in a nuclear war.[17] As evidence, proponents pointed to a Soviet network of hardened and buried bunkers that would allow key leadership to wage such a war.[18] They argued that this network had to be destroyed for the Soviet Union to be deterred.

Since the end of the Cold War, however, a rather different picture has emerged. While the Soviet leadership certainly valued its existence (as do all governments), the burrowing programme was actually a defensive step. The Soviet leadership worried that it lacked the ability to retaliate after a US first strike and so sought to protect itself in order to better deter the United States. Based on many interviews with senior Soviet leaders from the Cold War, a major 1995 study commissioned by the US Department of Defense concluded that

> Soviet provisions made for nuclear war, such as the network of well-hardened shelters, suggest much less an eagerness for armed conflict than pessimism about successful pre-emption of the U.S. and an expectation of the need for readiness to ride out a nuclear attack, as well as the vain hope of Politburo members to preserve their own lives and power.[19]

The study emphasised that 'Soviet political leaders appeared to grasp the danger posed by nuclear use, and they showed little real confidence in the USSR's ability to survive a nuclear war'.[20] If this was indeed the case, then the destruction of the Soviet leadership network was never necessary for deterrence; societal destruction would have been sufficient. This, in turn, casts serious doubt on contemporary claims, which stem directly from the latter part of the Cold War, that the threat of societal destruction might not be enough to deter contemporary Russia.

Also relevant is experience from the very early Cold War, when the United States had an extremely small nuclear arsenal: throughout the 1940s it numbered well under 500 warheads.[21] At that time, the US faced Joseph Stalin, arguably the most brutal dictator it has ever attempted to deter. Indeed, his supposed willingness to incur massive casualties during the Second World War was cited as key evidence by those who argued that the threat of city annihilation was not enough to deter the Soviet Union.[22] Moreover, Moscow was probably aware of the limited size of the US arsenal and believed that it would be used against 'the most important Soviet military–economic and administrative-political centers' (i.e., war-supporting industries and cities).[23] Whether nuclear weapons had a deterrent effect on Stalin is, therefore, highly relevant.

Superficially, there is evidence that the small size of the US arsenal did indeed detract from its deterrence value. Soviet military thinkers apparently believed that a small arsenal would not be decisive in the outcome of a war. Soviet-era historian David Holloway has pointed out that in about 1950, for instance, Soviet analysts (as well as, interestingly, their US counterparts) had concluded that 300 or so nuclear weapons – about the number the US possessed at that time – were insufficient to allow the US to defeat the Soviet Union.[24] He implies that this detracted from the deterrent value of the bomb.[25]

Yet, the real question is not whether nuclear weapons would have allowed the US to defeat the Soviet Union, but whether the pain the US could have inflicted, even in defeat, made war unattractive to Stalin. When the prospect of war was distant, Stalin was willing to behave aggressively to demonstrate that he was not cowed by the US nuclear monopoly (a challenge that no longer confronts Russian leaders).[26] However, on the one occasion during the late 1940s when there was even a remote possibility that events could escalate to the point where the US might consider using nuclear weapons, the Berlin Blockade of 1948–9, Stalin did not escalate the crisis. His unwillingness to attack the allied planes resupplying Berlin ultimately forced him to reopen access to Berlin in a humiliating climb-down.

There can be little doubt that, in the immediate aftermath of the Second World War, even a major non-nuclear war must have had a very significant deterrent value in its own right. But US nuclear weapons (of which there were only 110 in 1948) do appear to have played a significant role in deterring Stalin from escalating the crisis. Russian historian Victor Gobarev, based on archival evidence and interviews, has concluded that '[o]bjectively speaking, the US nuclear monopoly was the single most important factor which restrained Stalin's possible temptation to resolve the Berlin problem by military means'.[27] Western authors, although somewhat more cautious, generally agree.[28] What the available evidence cannot prove is that it was necessarily the threat of city destruction that deterred Stalin – it may have been the potential loss of his war-supporting industries. However, even at low numbers and after absorbing a first strike, the US would probably have little difficulty destroying significant fractions of both.[29]

If history, however, leads to the wrong conclusion and contemporary Russia (unlike the Soviet Union) really cannot be deterred by the threat of societal destruction, the question arises of how much Russian state power must be held at risk. During the Cold War, when the stakes were extremely high, it was argued that deterrence required the ability to destroy the Soviet state. However, in any conceivable conflict for the foreseeable future, the stake for Russia would almost certainly be much lower than it was during the Cold War. Therefore, the scale of damage the US needs to inflict – and the size of the arsenal it requires – should be correspondingly lower.[30] Indeed, this was the conclusion reached by the United States' closest ally, the United Kingdom, during the Cold War.[31] It shared the US assumption that the destruction of Soviet state power (not its citizens) was what counted, but it also believed that the USSR was sensitive to the stake involved. In consequence, it reached the conclusion that if the United States abandoned NATO in a crisis, the UK could deter the Soviet Union with a small arsenal since 'Overwhelming Britain would be a much smaller prize than overwhelming the United States, and a smaller prospective penalty could therefore suffice to tilt [the Soviet] assessment against starting aggression that would risk incurring the penalty'.[32]

Countervalue targeting

Noting that the case for the effectiveness of small arsenals hinges on the damage that even a few nuclear weapons can inflict upon cities, a second criticism of deep reductions often put forward by US commentators is that they would force a shift from counterforce targeting (that is, holding adversary nuclear forces at risk) to countervalue targeting (holding population centres at risk).[33] Such a shift is seen as undesirable because deliberate nuclear attacks on civilians are considered both incredible and immoral.

This argument is, however, misleading. Current US targeting policy is far from purely counterforce; as noted above, the target list, although focused on military targets, is much broader than just enemy nuclear forces. Some targets are close to major population centres and attacks on them would cause massive civilian casualties (irrespective of the purpose of the attack).[34] Indeed, given the analysis in the previous section, nuclear deterrence probably stems primarily from the collateral damage that would inevitably accompany a nuclear strike. The deterrent value of collateral damage is, however, effectively ignored in current US targeting policy.[35] One option for the US in developing war plans against China and Russia at low numbers would, therefore, be to focus on a subset of existing targets, including leadership, military-industrial targets and conventional military facilities, and simply recognise that the collateral damage inflicted by these attacks significantly enhances deterrence.[36] This strategy would not create new moral problems or reduce credibility (provided that some limited options for the escalation phase of a crisis were available).

Russia and tactical nuclear weapons

A third criticism of deep reductions, that large numbers of tactical nuclear weapons are required to offset conventional inferiority, is generally made by Russians. (Tactical nuclear weapons, as discussed in the Appendix, are a broad and somewhat arbitrarily defined class of nuclear weapons that include short-range weapons for 'battlefield' use.) In public, Russian analysts express concern about the conventional balance in Europe and link this issue to tactical nuclear arms control.[37] Over the long term, however, a greater concern appears to be the challenge of defending its vast southeastern frontier against a conventionally superior China in the event that Sino-Russian relations sour.[38] Moreover, Russia lags behind the US in long-range high-precision conventional weapons. Some in Russia argue that its tactical nuclear forces provide a counterbalance, a point that is overlooked in much of the Western discourse about Russia's views on tactical nuclear weapons.[39] Indeed, in remarks to the State Duma in January 2010, Russian Foreign Minister Sergey Lavrov linked tactical nuclear arms control to a number of other areas including the conventional balance in Europe and 'non-nuclear strategic weapons'.[40]

Deep reductions would force Russia to abandon most of, but not all, its tactical nuclear weapons. Whether the tens that might remain would appear sufficient to Russia depend very much on doctrine. If tactical nuclear weapons are viewed as tools for deterrence by denial – for physically defeating, and hence deterring, a Chinese invasion across a border stretching over 3,500km – hundreds of them might be needed. A 1 kT nuclear explosion would, however, release at least 70 times more radioactivity than the Chernobyl disaster (although the radiation from the former would decay much more quickly than that from the latter has).[41] The large-scale use of tactical nuclear weapons on or close to Russian soil therefore lacks credibility and does little to enhance deterrence, over and above their limited use. Similarly, the concept of using tactical nuclear weapons as some sort of direct substitute for high-precision conventional weapons is frankly incredible.

There is, however, an alternative conception for 'tactical' nuclear weapons: their use very sparingly at the start of a conflict for the 'strategic' purpose of signalling resolve by increasing the risk of escalation.[42] If this is the Russian concept of tactical nuclear weapons, and Russian analysts often stress that it is, then even tens of them should be sufficient for deterrence (if not for satisfying Russian domestic demand for a visible manifestation of its great-power status). Whether a specific category of short-range nuclear weapons designated as tactical is really needed for this purpose is debatable. In particular, it is far from clear that responding to US high-precision conventional weapons with nuclear weapons could be even remotely credible. However, such issues are moot, since retaining a few tens of tactical nuclear weapons would not be a barrier to deep reductions.

CHAPTER TWO

Extended deterrence

The United States is committed to deterring aggression against its allies as well as against itself. In doing so it does not rule out the use of nuclear weapons. Indeed, it has recently been unusually explicit in emphasising the availability of nuclear options in fulfilling its security guarantees towards Japan and South Korea.[1] Although other nuclear-armed states do have defence commitments, including through NATO and the Collective Security Treaty Organization, and they may extend deterrence US-style to allies in future, extended deterrence today is a mission particular to the United States.

There can be little doubt that, as a matter of politics, extended deterrence will complicate deep reductions. Assuring allies has generally been a more difficult task than deterring their enemies. Historically, the US has used both the overall size of its arsenal as well as specific capabilities for 'assurance'. Moreover, some allies have a visceral feeling that when it comes to nuclear weapons 'more is better'. In consequence, some allies, especially Japan and certain newer NATO member states, are wary of deep reductions (although all are internally divided on the issue).[2]

Resistance may be lessened if the US continually reempha-
sises that it will maintain parity with Russia and a numerical
advantage over China. Much may depend on the path to low
numbers. For instance, some Eastern European allies of the US
have expressed concern about the possibility of the United
States withdrawing the 200 or so B61 gravity bombs that are
deployed in Europe. However, NATO has unanimously agreed
that any further reductions 'must take into account the dispar-
ity with the greater Russian stockpiles of short-range nuclear
weapons'.[3] Indeed, even staunch critics of unilateral with-
drawal support a reciprocal NATO–Russia process, recognising
that reducing the total number of nuclear weapons in Europe
would enhance security.[4] Of course, it would be unrealistic
to expect there to be no concern on the part of any ally about
deep reductions; the reality is that even if the US handles alliance politics more deftly than it has in the past – and the 2010
Nuclear Posture Review suggests it might – allies' concerns will
probably act as a brake. However, the scale of allies' concerns is
likely to be rather path dependent.[5]

The operative question here, however, is whether, from a
strategic perspective, deep reductions would actually make
extended deterrence less viable. There is a widely held assumption that the United States needs a large nuclear arsenal, if not
outright strategic superiority, to credibly extend deterrence to
its allies.[6] The key theoretical argument for this proposition is
damage limitation. Others are considered in Chapter Five.

Damage limitation

The central challenge with extended deterrence is ensuring
that US nuclear threats on behalf of an ally are credible. Some
US allies worry that, in some circumstances, they might not be.
Although officials rarely voice this concern (probably for fear
of offending the US), one more forthright Japanese analyst has

argued that 'if North Korea or China could retain a sufficient capability to strike the US homeland, the United States would not be willing to sacrifice its security for the sake of its allies' security'.[7]

European (and Asian) allies' concerns during the Cold War were identical. Critics of mutual assured destruction worried that it was an incredible basis on which to extend deterrence. They argued that, for its threats to be credible, the US had to significantly limit the damage it would suffer in a nuclear war on behalf of an ally.[8] Large arsenals with significant counter-force capabilities were advocated as a way of achieving this. Missile defences (and to a lesser extent civil defences) were also advocated but always suffered from severe practical limitations, such as the technical challenge of reliably intercepting incoming ballistic missiles and the logistical challenges of sheltering literally millions of people for prolonged periods.

For essentially identical reasons, damage limitation capabilities were also argued by some deterrence theorists to be important during the 'escalation phase' of a crisis. Early in a crisis the protagonists may engage in brinkmanship, that is, taking progressively larger risks to demonstrate their commitment to a cause in the hope that the other will back down. By reducing the costs of nuclear war, it was argued, damage limitation capabilities both emboldened American brinkmanship and undermined the will of an adversary.

The specific term 'damage limitation' was excised from the official American strategic lexicon in the late 1960s and, at about the same time, many US analysts rejected the concept too.[9] However, among some allies and analysts, damage limitation (even if that specific term is not always used) is still a major justification for the need to retain large arsenals.

One Japanese analyst, for instance, argued as recently as 2002 that damage limitation is 'key to increasing the credibility of the threat of nuclear use'.[10] A 2010 report by the National Institute for Defense Studies, the Japanese Ministry of Defense's in-house think tank, develops this line of thought, arguing that, for extended deterrence to be credible, US capabilities for escalation control

> must be underpinned by a superior damage-limiting capability made possible by a strong counterforce capability against the potential aggressor (the ability to effectively destroy the enemy's nuclear strike force) and an effective strategic defense force. This is because, if the damage-limiting capability of the country providing the nuclear umbrella is superior to that of the aggressor, its threat to embark on a nuclear retaliation and nuclear exchanges will be all the more credible and its deterrent effect all the stronger.[11]

In addition, some civilian strategists continue to argue for the importance of damage limitation. In 2009, the Congressionally mandated US Strategic Posture Commission argued that 'the United States must also design its strategic forces with the objective of being able to limit damage from an attacker if a war begins'.[12] The commission did not indicate whether this recommendation related to a nuclear war with any state in particular. However, since the end of the Cold War, authors (including at least one member of the commission) have argued the US needs to be able to limit damage in a nuclear war with China.[13]

There is little evidence that US civilian leaders place much, if any, importance on damage limitation any more. Indeed, in 2006, current and former senior Pentagon officials vehemently denied claims that the United States was striving to develop the capability to execute a 'splendid' first strike against Russia (something that would be a potentially important component of a damage-limitation strategy).[14] However, the US military may still regard the ability to limit damage in a nuclear war as important. Leaving aside the natural desire on the part of military planners to reduce the damage to the US should deterrence fail, damage limitation may still be seen as a way to enhance deterrence. For instance, the US military's 2006 *Deterrence Operations: Joint Operating Concept* states that the

> key challenge to improving the effectiveness of deterrence by cost imposition is to overcome adversary perceptions that they can successfully deter US attack, or that the US will be self-deterred. Improved offensive and defensive damage limitation capabilities for the US homeland, allies, non-combatants, and forward-deployed forces are essential to addressing this challenge.[15]

Also potentially revealing is the oft-heard remark that deep reductions would force the US to change from counterforce to countervalue targeting. This comment makes little sense from the perspective of US declaratory policy, which, as noted above, has consistently advocated counterforce targeting as a punishment strategy. In fact, what this remark might mean is that as numbers decrease it would become increasingly difficult to meet the targeting requirements for a damage-limitation strategy because such a strategy probably requires targeting not only weapons but also command and control facilities and leadership bunkers to try to prevent undestroyed weapons from being used.

High-precision conventional munitions are increasingly being integrated into US operational plans and are taking over some missions from nuclear weapons.[16] However, their capability against hardened targets is still very limited and likely to remain so. (Besides, they are currently only envisaged as a niche capability, not intended to upset strategic stability with China or Russia).[17] Thus, until ballistic-missile defences are much improved, damage limitation – especially against China and Russia – would seem to rely on retaining a sizeable nuclear arsenal.

How effective is damage limitation?

Russia's nuclear force is much more capable than China's and much harder to destroy. In consequence, if the option of attempting a damage-limiting strike against China adds nothing to deterrence, it certainly adds nothing against Russia. Scenarios involving China are, therefore, the most important for assessing the effect of deep reductions on extended deterrence.

Much has been made recently about the vulnerability of China's silo-based missiles.[18] However, for exactly this reason, China's focus, for some time now, has been on developing sea-based and land-based mobile systems. According to the 2010 edition of *Military and Security Developments Involving the People's Republic of China*, published by the US Department of Defense, China currently has between about 95 and 120 transporter-erector-launchers (TELs) for a similar number of nuclear-armed ballistic missiles.[19] Although 'only' around 10–15 of them can hit the continental United States, all of them can hit allies such as Taiwan or Japan (where, for instance, the US Seventh Fleet is based), as a US president would be painfully aware in a crisis. (By comparison, Russia currently has about 170 road-mobile ICBMs that could hit the United States and it is building more.[20] As its total arsenal comes down it is likely to prioritise this basing mode yet further.)

Destroying dispersed road-mobile missiles is much harder than destroying silos.[21] They must be located and then successfully attacked very quickly (before they can be relocated). The US ability to destroy mobile missiles has increased considerably since the 1991 Gulf War, when the US failed to score a single confirmed kill of a mobile SCUD TEL in 1,460 sorties directed against missile-related targets.[22] Indeed, to demonstrate what might be possible, proponents of damage limitation could point to the example of Israel, in its 2006 war in Lebanon, in which it destroyed about 80–90% of Hizbullah's 125 or so medium- and long-range TELs.[23]

However, even if the United States achieved a similar success rate against China, as many as 25 Chinese TELs might survive to launch a counterstrike. In reality, for at least five reasons, it is extremely unlikely that the US would be nearly as successful against China as Israel was against Hizbullah. Firstly, and most importantly, the US would have to strike Chinese TELs virtually simultaneously to preclude the possibility of Chinese nuclear retaliation once it realised a US first strike was under way. Although Israel reportedly destroyed over 50 TELs in less than 40 minutes, it took a further two days to destroy the next 50.[24] Furthermore, Israel located a number of Hizbullah's TELs by detecting the rockets they had launched; if the US wanted to limit the damage from nuclear-armed missiles, it would have to find some way of detecting all Chinese TELs prior to the launch of their missiles. A third distinction is that China's Second Artillery (its military force responsible for nuclear weapons) is surely much more adept and practised at hiding mobile missiles than Hizbullah. Hiding TELs in China's vast land mass is intrinsically easier than hiding them in much smaller Lebanon. In addition, the UAVs and aircraft that were central to the Israeli effort would have to operate in a much more hostile environment over China.

In addition to these five factors, there is significant uncertainty (of about 20% based on the data in *Military and Security*

Developments Involving the People's Republic of China) in how many TELs and nuclear-armed ballistic missiles China possesses. Without knowing how many TELs it must locate, the US could have no confidence that it had successfully tracked them all, thus increasing the uncertainty associated with attacking them. (Israel, of course, faced the same problem but it mattered far less because Hizbullah's missiles were conventional.)

Two potential methods of destroying dispersed mobile missiles have been proposed. The classic 'Cold War' solution would be a 'barrage' attack using a large number of relatively high-yield nuclear weapons to destroy all the mobile missiles (along with anything else that happened to be present) across a large area. Advocates of damage limitation generally do not endorse this approach, since they are concerned with reducing collateral damage to enhance the credibility of nuclear use. Lieber and Press, for instance, advocate a more targeted approach. They argue that the use of 'low-yield nuclear weapons would significantly reduce the targeting problem; locating the launchers within half a mile would suffice if a five-kiloton warhead were used'.[25] A mobile missile could, however, move half a mile from its point of discovery within about two minutes.[26] The only way one could be targeted in such a short time would be from planes (or conceivably nuclear-armed UAVs or retargetable cruise missiles) carrying nuclear weapons and loitering over Chinese airspace. A missile launched from outside Chinese airspace could not reach the target in time. Given the number of planes that would be required to simultaneously cover the vast potential roaming grounds of Chinese mobile missiles, the refueling capability to support these planes and hostile actions by Chinese air-defence units, such a strategy is utterly impractical. Moreover, the arrival of this airborne armada would give China clear warning that a US nuclear strike was imminent.

Moreover, China's deterrent may have been bolstered slightly by its development of the *Jin*-class SSBN. Two submarines in this class have been built and more are under construction.[27] A 2009 report from the US Office of Naval Intelligence describes China's SSBN force as the country's 'first credible second-strike nuclear capability'.[28] This is an odd statement given that China's road-mobile missile force already represents a credible second-strike capability and the Office of Naval Intelligence's own assessment that *Jin*-class SSBNs are noisier than Soviet *Delta* III-class SSBNs (first deployed in 1976) and hence probably vulnerable to US anti-submarine warfare operations.[29] Nevertheless, the report would appear to indicate that the US navy cannot guarantee its ability to eliminate all Chinese SSBNs before they were able to launch at least one missile.[30]

Ballistic-missile defences are sometimes advocated as a solution to this morass of problems. It is argued that if the United States could destroy most Chinese ballistic missiles using kinetic weapons, defences (especially if they were significantly expanded) might allow it to 'mop up' the remainder after launch.[31] Defences, however, suffer from significant limitations. If China could destroy the radars on which ballistic-missile defence systems rely – as it would surely try to do – it could render them completely inoperable. Moreover, ballistic-missile defences are unlikely to be 'cost effective at the margins', that is, China could probably develop countermeasures much more cheaply and quickly than the US could build or improve interceptors.[32] Indeed, *Military and Security Developments Involving the People's Republic of China* notes that

China is also currently working on a range of technologies to attempt to counter U.S. and other militaries' ballistic missile defense systems, including maneuvering re-entry vehicles, [MIRVs], decoys, chaff, jamming, thermal shielding, and anti-satellite (ASAT) weapons.[33]

Finally, ballistic-missile defences are only useful for defeating nuclear weapons delivered by ballistic missile. China has between 200 and 500 DH-10 cruise missiles that could hit Taiwan or US forces in theatre.[34] These missiles are currently armed with conventional warheads, but if China ever became really worried about US ballistic-missile defences, it could, given time, arm them with nuclear warheads, complicating a US first strike yet further.[35]

In summary, a US damage-limiting strike against China would in all probability only be partially effective. Against Russia the challenges are even greater. Even if the US could somehow limit damage in a nuclear war against either adversary to the (probably unattainable) level of five American or allied cities, a decision-maker following the Bundy model would probably not regard such a war as being significantly more attractive. If, more plausibly, the damage were tens of cities, the same would probably also be true for a decision-maker following the Kahn model. Moreover, the result of a damage-limiting strike would also be highly uncertain, and this is likely to significantly reduce the attractiveness of executing one.

Damage-limitation capabilities might still work to the United States' advantage if an adversary wrongly believed that the US had a credible first-strike option. In this case, the adversary might be deterred from brinkmanship, providing the United States with a net advantage. It is impossible to know whether a US adversary would deem a US first strike to be a realistic possibility. In the middle of a deep crisis, Beijing or Moscow could decide that the US might attempt a first strike in spite of the myriad risks outlined above. However, this belief comes at a very high price: a significant increase in crisis instability. As described below, the potential for crisis instability is sufficiently serious that the US should actually not want to undermine the survivability of China's or Russia's forces.

Ultimately, when it comes to deterring aggression by China or Russia against allies, the credibility of US extended guarantees is likely to remain the willingness to absorb very high costs, rather than the ability to lower those costs. Whether damage limitation could make more of a difference against states armed with very small arsenals – such as North Korea or a putative nuclear-armed Iran – is more of an open question. There is certainly a somewhat stronger (though by no means watertight) argument that in such cases a damage-limiting strike could be credible and would enhance deterrence. However, at the warhead levels considered in this study, this would simply not be an issue; reductions to 500 warheads would almost certainly not force the United States to change its current nuclear strategy, except in regard to China and Russia.

Looking back: the Berlin Crisis

The Berlin Crisis of 1958–62 is the key case study for assessing this critique of damage limitation. Firstly, because of the Soviet Union's local conventional superiority, US threats to guarantee the status of West Berlin ultimately rested on nuclear weapons. Secondly, at the time of the crisis, the United States had a large arsenal capable of very significant damage limitation. Thirdly, the stakes were extremely high for both sides; this was probably the closest the United States has ever been to nuclear war over one of its own foreign security commitments. Lastly, received wisdom about the perceived requirements for extended deterrence may have stemmed, in large part, from the successful outcome of the crisis.[36]

Nikita Khrushchev sparked the Berlin Crisis in November 1958 when he threatened to sign a peace treaty with East Germany and, in the process, transfer to it all responsibility for decisions about access to West Berlin. This declaration was tantamount to annexing West Berlin. The Soviet Union stated its intention to delay this action for six months to allow negotiations. An almost identical set of demands was issued in June 1961.

Khrushchev's failure to enact his threats suggests he was deterred.[37] In fact, even his most provocative act, the construction of the Berlin Wall in August 1961, provides evidence for the effectiveness of US deterrent threats. The wall did not violate any of the explicit red lines set out by President Kennedy in a key speech of July 25. Despite the urging of East German leader Walter Ulbricht, Khrushchev did not authorise the closure of the air corridors into West Berlin, which were the subject of a specific written agreement.[38] Moreover, Khrushchev even appeared ready to back down if construction of the wall had met with resistance. He told Ulbricht to first use barbed wire to seal the border and emphasised that 'no decision regarding a wall would be taken until it could be determined with accuracy how the Western powers would respond to this measure'.[39]

Did deterrence depend on the United States' large arsenal? The fact of US nuclear superiority does not answer this question by itself. Rather, it is necessary to examine the decision-making of both sides to assess whether the United States was emboldened by its large arsenal to engage in effective brinkmanship; and whether inferiority weakened the USSR.

On the first issue, there is considerable evidence that American officials believed that US damage-limitation capabilities did not make a difference. In the summer of 1961, Carl Kaysen, a Harvard economist then serving as a special assistant to National Security Adviser Bundy, led a study that examined the feasibility of a US first strike designed to eliminate Soviet long-range nuclear weapons but limit collateral damage. (The contemporary war plan, SIOP-62, included huge attacks against urban-industrial targets.)[40] Kaysen's study predicted that after a US first strike 'only a few' of almost 1,650 megatons of Soviet long-range weaponry would survive.[41] The number of Americans killed in a possible Soviet counter-strike would, therefore, be 'small percentage-wise': between 5 million and 13 million. However, potential retaliation on this scale did not make a nuclear war appear less unattractive and the plan was quickly dropped.[42] On this occasion, the ability to limit damage in the event of war did little to enhance US resolve (consistent with the Bundy model of decision-making). The success of US brinkmanship is thus better explained by its willingness to absorb high costs, apparently because Kennedy regarded Berlin as a test case for the credibility of all US defence commitments and believed that national security hinged on those commitments.

Interestingly, having been briefed on the plan in September 1961, Kennedy observed to his generals that a surprise attack aimed at destroying the long-range striking power of the USSR would leave a sizable number of MRBMs [medium-range ballistic missiles] facing Europe, and he asked about options for attempting to nullify this threat.[43] Neither the Soviet MRBM force, nor its potential effect on Europe, had been considered in Kaysen's study. This point is significant because it demonstrates that, in a crisis, a president would be intensely aware of the threat to allied cities, something that is often forgotten by contemporary advocates of damage limitation who tend to focus only on the requirements for eliminating Chinese and Russian ICBMs and not their shorter-range systems.

US nuclear superiority does not appear to have constrained Khrushchev's actions. Khrushchev sparked the crisis in 1958, and then reignited it in 1961, in spite of US nuclear superiority. He did so because he believed that the damage that could be wrought to Western Europe with 'literally several bombs' would cause the United States to back down, a point he made to the Polish leader Wladylsaw Gomulka shortly before he issued his 1958 ultimatum.[44] He made the same argument to the Soviet Presidium on 26 May 1961 in making the case for a second ultimatum, and again on 2 July 1961 to the British ambassador in Moscow.[45] In effect, Khrushchev was arguing that American sensitivity to civilian casualties negated its counterforce damage-limitation capabilities. Moreover, based on recently opened Soviet archives, historian Vladislav Zubok has concluded that, in contrast to his public statements, Khrushchev 'did not even talk about the nuclear balance' in private.[46] Khrushchev's belief that the nuclear balance did not matter appears to have been correct. His mistake was his failure to appreciate the importance the United States placed on Berlin.

Extended deterrence and conventional power

Today, a US president would still be unlikely to view damage limitation as effective enough to significantly lower the perceived costs of a nuclear war against China or Russia. However, what makes extended deterrence easier than during the Berlin Crisis is the rise of US conventional power. The conventional balance affects extended deterrence much more than central deterrence. In the words of one Japanese diplomat, US conventional superiority 'obviates the whole debate about whether or not Washington would "sacrifice Los Angeles to save Tokyo" in a nuclear exchange'.[47]

The effects of US conventional superiority are, perhaps, most marked on the Korean Peninsula. Although both Japan and South Korea are clearly and understandably worried about North Korea and its non-conventional weapons programmes, there is little doubt that US and South Korean forces would prevail in a conflict against North Korea. The US would certainly want to keep the use of nuclear weapons on the table to deter their use by North Korea. However, only a few would be required for this purpose. Crucially, there is no case for using large numbers of nuclear weapons tactically to destroy North Korean ballistic missiles or artillery quickly in order to reduce the damage inflicted on Japan and South Korea in the time required to defeat North Korea. The proximity of Seoul and other South Korean population centres to the North Korean border would necessitate using as few nuclear weapons as possible to minimise fallout. Moreover, the mobility of North Korean short-range ballistic missiles places a premium on reconnaissance, not fire power.

US conventional superiority is, however, probably not as marked today as some believe. Conventional deterrence depends much more on the local than the global balance of forces.[48] Area-denial capabilities – such as anti-ship ballistic missiles that could limit US freedom of action in vital regions – are being sought by China in particular. These have important consequences for extended deterrence in East Asia. Similarly, cyber-attack and anti-satellite capabilities can affect the information gathering and processing operations that are central to US conventional power. Moreover, both the US and its allies worry that US conventional superiority is on the wane. The question, therefore, arises of whether the US could offset any conventional weaknesses that surface in future by retaining more nuclear weapons.

Would a larger US nuclear arsenal help offset conventional weaknesses?

Once the concept of damage limitation as a one-size-fits-all means of bolstering credibility has been discarded, it is instructive to examine possible extended deterrence challenges on a case-by-case basis to assess whether more nuclear weapons might help mitigate future conventional weakness. Of most immediate concern is the challenge of deterring China from 'subduing' Taiwan, were the latter to declare independence. Although the United States has made it clear privately to both China and Taiwan that its security guarantee holds only so long as Taiwan does not declare independence, a US president might still decide to intervene. This would be much harder if China could deny the US Seventh Fleet access to the Taiwan Strait; then nuclear options could come into play.[49]

Over the longer term, if China shifted its focus from area denial to power projection, the US and its allies would start worrying about a broader range of scenarios. China might attempt to use force to settle simmering disputes with Japan, such as the ownership of the uninhabited Senkaku/Diaoyu islands or the right to exploit disputed gas fields in the East China Sea. In these scenarios, however, nuclear use would be extremely unlikely (although if a US carrier were sunk it might not be completely unimaginable). More relevant for nuclear planning is the possibility of an invasion of Taiwan, were China ever to attain the degree of conventional superiority necessary to contemplate a D-Day-style operation. Likewise, nuclear threats could also be relevant in Europe, were a revanchist Russia to make an attempt to seize territory from a NATO member state, most probably one of the Baltic states.

In all of these scenarios any type of nuclear threat would probably lack credibility and, as a result, the US and its allies should strive to prevent China and Russia attaining local conventional dominance. If, however, the US lost conventional superiority, the central challenge facing it would, as always, be how to convince China and Russia that it might actually use nuclear weapons in the defence of an ally. More nuclear weapons would not help. In particular, using significant numbers of tactical nuclear weapons on or close to an ally's territory, even to retard an invasion, lacks credibility for the reasons discussed above.

The most credible nuclear threats the US could make would probably be against conventional military assets on Chinese or Russian territory, such as airbases, naval docks or logistics nodes that were supporting the invasion. The purpose of such attacks would not be tactical (in the sense that their primary aim was to interfere with the invasion) but strategic: to show resolve by increasing the chance of escalation. Large numbers of nuclear weapons would be unnecessary for this purpose. It is unclear whether such potential adversaries would view such a strategy as credible. However, the onus should be on those that assert that deep reductions would undermine extended deterrence to demonstrate how large numbers of nuclear weapons could enhance the credibility of nuclear threats made by a conventionally inferior power.

CHAPTER THREE

Crisis stability

The only circumstance in which the deliberate use of a nuclear weapon by Russia or the United States is conceivable would be in the midst of a deep crisis. Ensuring that such a crisis is stable – that no state has an incentive to use nuclear weapons because it fears that an opponent is about to do so – is critically important. Many potential causes of crisis instability (such as emotion, pressure, bad advice, miscalculation, misperception or poor communication) have little to do with arsenal size. However, crisis instability can be exacerbated by the interaction of vulnerable forces on one side with counterforce and defensive capabilities on the other. This could lead the state with vulnerable forces to attack pre-emptively to avoid being pre-empted. This specific type of crisis instability, a direct result of force posture, known as first-strike instability, could be exacerbated by deep reductions.

Deep reductions by Russia and the United States would be unlikely to have much of an impact on stability in a crisis involving one of them and another nation. The critical question is their effect on the stability of US–Russian crises. Probably the biggest danger arises from the possibility that Russia might use nuclear weapons first out of the (almost certainly mistaken) belief that the US was about to do so. As the stronger conventional power, the US would have the most to lose if nuclear weapons were introduced into a conflict. However, faced with the United States' impressive nuclear capability, Moscow might wrongly infer a willingness to use it. For instance, even Russians not prone to flights of fancy in interpreting American policy concluded that the Bush administration created an 'increased focus of doctrines on nuclear deterrence (including pre-emptive and preventive use of nuclear weapons)'.[1] Bush administration officials may rightly argue this was a serious misrepresentation of their policy. However, from the perspective of stability, it does not really matter whether Russian beliefs about American doctrine are misrepresentations or not; it is manifestly not in the US interest for Russia to believe mistakenly that the US would be likely to use nuclear weapons pre-emptively.

If, in a crisis, Russia comes to believe that a US nuclear attack is likely, it could launch a large-scale first strike to try to limit the damage it would suffer. However, there are two other options it could take, which are probably more likely.[2] Firstly, it might decide to use nuclear weapons on a smaller scale out of the belief that doing so would terrify the US into backing down. In particular, it might calculate that the limited use of nuclear weapons would coerce the American population into demanding its government cease hostilities immediately. Whether this strategy would work is essentially immaterial; the issue here is simply that, out of desperation, Russia might try it. Secondly, Russia could take takes steps to enhance the survivability of its forces, but by dispersing its mobile delivery systems it would risk sending (possibly unintended) escalatory signals, which might in turn raise the 'temperature' of crisis and increase the chance of further escalation leading to nuclear use. It is in Russia and the United States' interests to avoid all of these eventualities.

Russian concerns

The key to ensuring first-strike stability is survivable nuclear forces. Today, Russia is concerned about the survivability of its forces.[3] Part of this concern relates to its silo-based ICBMs, which, as described further in the Appendix (p. 101), are loaded with multiple warheads. Given that the United States would probably target each Russian silo with two warheads, a US strike on Russian ICBMs would destroy significantly more warheads than it consumed. This problem has existed for as long as ICBMs have been armed with MIRVs but, in Russian eyes, it has been exacerbated by the US development of conventional precision-guided munitions, including guided gravity bombs, cruise missiles and prompt global strike (which is a nascent programme to develop high-precision conventional weapons capable of being delivered anywhere in the world in less than an hour). Russia worries that such weapons are increasingly able to hold its silos (and its command and control system) at risk.[4] Some in Russia have even started to ask whether the US could be deterred from launching a conventional first strike against Russian ICBMs.[5] Because such a strike would lead to almost no civilian casualties, they worry that a Russian nuclear response would lack credibility. While the notion of a conventional first strike appears utterly fanciful to almost all analysts and officials in the US, it illustrates the depth of Russian concern.

The United States also holds a substantial lead in anti-submarine warfare and is trying to develop the ability to hold road-mobile ballistic missiles at risk.[6] Although current programmes are aimed primarily at conventional missiles in regional conflicts, Moscow is concerned that these foreshadow a capability against Russia.[7] It further worries that ballistic-missile defences – if they are developed and greatly expanded – might enable the US to 'mop up' the warheads it cannot destroy in a first strike.[8] Repeated American protestations that Russia is not the target of its ballistic-missile defence efforts have done little to ease Russian concerns. The new 'Phased Adaptive Approach' for Europe, unveiled by the Obama administration in September 2009, has made more of a difference. The Ground-Based Midcourse Interceptors that the Bush administration had planned to deploy in Europe were designed to target missiles with intermediate and intercontinental ranges. The Phased Adaptive Approach, by contrast, is focused – at least in its initial stages – on countering the shorter-range missile threat from Iran and the Standard Missile 3 interceptors that will be deployed in Europe over the course of this decade are simply incapable of intercepting Russian ICBMs. However, as Russian Foreign Minister Sergey Lavrov emphasised in 2010, at the conclusion of New START, Russia is concerned for the long term because the US intends to develop the Standard Missile 3 interceptor so that, by around 2020, it has some capability to counter ICBMs.[9]

To be clear, in spite of Russian protestations, the Russian government and military is fully aware of the extraordinary challenges facing the United States if it ever wanted to execute a first strike. However, there is a genuine fear that deep reductions, coupled with significant technological developments, could completely undermine the survivability of Russia's nuclear forces. Indeed, senior Russian officials, including Lavrov and the ambassador to the US, Sergei Kislyak, have made it very clear that arms reductions beyond New START are contingent upon their concerns being addressed.[10] These concerns are broader than crisis stability. Moscow's primary worry is that if its deterrent is compromised it might become unable to deter the US from infringing upon Russian vital interests. What should potentially concern the United States is that if such concerns generate crisis instability, US security might be negatively affected too.

How much of a problem is crisis instability?

Looking forward, Russian fears are exaggerated. The US appears highly unlikely to develop a realistic first-strike option for the foreseeable future, even at low numbers. Ballistic-missile defences against ICBMs have yet to be tested, let alone proven, in realistic conditions. As described above, against a practised and sophisticated adversary, such as Russia, destroying dispersed road-mobile missiles is fiendishly difficult. Moreover, even if US attack submarines could tail all Russian SSBNs, the US navy could not confidently destroy all of them before their first weapons were launched. Given any US president's aversion to sustaining even a very limited nuclear attack against the United States, it seems unlikely, even at low numbers, that a first strike against Russia could ever appear to be an attractive option. In fact, it is striking that a major concern in the United States and amongst its allies, discussed in the previous section, that damage-limitation would become even harder at low numbers, is the exact opposite of Russian fears. (Exactly why Russia and the US have reached such different conclusions is not clear, but worst-case thinking on each side appears to be partly to blame).

In spite of all of this, there are both political and strategic reasons for taking Russian concerns seriously. Firstly, Russia will not agree to deep reductions unless its concerns are addressed. At points during New START negotiations, Russia tried to curtail US missile defence. This strategy was unsuccessful in practical terms but did not prove a deal breaker because New START reductions are relatively modest and because the US did accommodate other Russian concerns (by agreeing, for example, to count conventionally armed ballistic missiles as nuclear armed). Nevertheless, Russia is extremely unlikely to agree to a more ambitious follow-on treaty unless its concerns are more fully addressed.

Secondly, the absence of a credible American first-strike option against Russia is not a sufficient condition for first-strike stability. The belief that the United States had a credible first-strike option, even if such a belief were erroneous, could still lead to needless nuclear use in a crisis. Although the 2010 US Nuclear Posture Review recognises Russian concerns,[11] many American analysts and officials, particularly in Congress, are more dismissive. There is strong domestic opposition to the idea that stability concerns should be allowed to derail the development of technologies like missile defence that, some argue, are needed to defeat threats from 'undeterrable' states like Iran and North Korea.

What should give pause to those who show little sympathy for Russian concerns is the American experience. Contemporary Russian fears almost exactly mirror US fears from the late 1970s and early 1980s. Under the so-called Nitze scenario, propounded around that time, the United States would supposedly be deterred from responding to a 'clinical' Soviet first strike on US ICBMs by the threat of Soviet retaliation on US cities.[12] With the benefit of hindsight, we now know these fears were unfounded: the supposed 'window of vulnerability', during which the Soviet Union would have been able to eliminate the US ICBM force without fear of retaliation, simply did not exist.[13] Concern was nonetheless genuine.

To make matters worse, in the early 1980s, Soviet leaders became deeply concerned about a US first strike. These fears reached their height during NATO's 1983 *Able Archer* exercise, when the Soviet leadership may have alerted some of their nuclear forces.[14] US Defense Secretary Robert M. Gates (then a CIA analyst), has described *Able Archer* as 'one of the potentially most dangerous episodes of the Cold War',[15] adding: 'There is a good chance – with all of the other events in 1983 – that [Soviet leaders] really felt a NATO attack was at least possible and that they took a number of measures to enhance their military readiness short of mobilization.'[16] American and Russian concerns together could have compounded to create potentially catastrophic instability at this point, had a crisis of the same order of magnitude as those of the 1950s or early 1960s arisen.

One of these crises, the Cuban Missile Crisis, provides a concrete example of how the fear of a first strike can generate instability (albeit instability that ended short of major conflict). By mid-1962, Khrushchev had reversed his earlier belief about the irrelevance of the nuclear balance. In particular, he seems to have incorrectly concluded that US strategic superiority had emboldened it during the Berlin Crisis. The turning point may have been in March 1962 when he learned that the US had considered a first strike the previous summer. This may have 'stirred fears that the Americans were eager to capitalize on their strategic advantage'.[17] His subsequent decision to place missiles in Cuba sparked the most serious crisis of the Cold War. Thus, even conceding that strategic superiority was probably advantageous to the US during the Cuban Missile Crisis (because it may have contributed to Khrushchev backing down), it undermined US security on balance by helping to precipitate the crisis in the first place.[18]

Given the ongoing possibility of crises involving Russia and the United States, the need to maintain first-strike stability should shape the path – and, if necessary, restrain the pace – of deep reductions. In fact, even without further reductions, if Russian survivability concerns are not addressed, they could undermine stability. Although the probability of a nuclear exchange resulting from first-strike instability is low, its costs to both Russia and the US would be extremely high. Another possibility is that Russian survivability concerns could prompt it to rearm. The US should certainly want to avoid this eventuality.

Managing Russia's fears

It is beyond the scope of this study to explore in much detail the arms-control and confidence-building measures that might be required to reassure Russia.[19] However, three points bear emphasising. Firstly, more than mere words will be required. Russian officials worry that there can be a significant gap between US declaratory policy and its war plans. This concern was reflected by Ambassador Kislyak in remarks about the 2010 Nuclear Posture Review. He specifically declined to 'hail' the document in spite of its emphasis on strategic stability with Russia, saying: 'We have to see how it's going to be implemented in real life, how it is going to be translated into the force deployment and how it is going to be translated into cooperation… .'[20] Formal arms control with Russia will, therefore, be an important element in convincing it of American good faith.

Secondly, for the foreseeable future, any remotely plausible US first-strike option, even at low numbers, could only derive from a combination of technologies, not from any one individual technology. Therefore, addressing Russians concerns need not, as some analyses have claimed, involve eliminating ballistic-missile defence and banning prompt global strike and curtailing advanced surveillance capabilities and limiting anti-submarine warfare.[21] Rather, some limits on some of these technologies would be required (although getting agreement between Russia and the US on exactly what is needed will probably prove extremely difficult). However, even partial measures might well encounter domestic opposition in the United States, and Senate ratification could be challenging. For example, some American critics of arms control seized upon New START's extremely minimal regulation of ballistic-missile defence (it forbids the conversion of ICBM silos into interceptor silos and vice versa) as a way to attack the treaty.[22] The US Senate, in its resolution of ratification, emphasised that it could not accept any further limits. This is potentially problematic because an agreement to cap the size of an American anti-ballistic missile system could be a powerful way of convincing Russia that it is not the target of US defences.

Thirdly, the single most important step that could be taken to enhance first-strike stability would be to work once again towards eliminating ICBMs armed with multiple warheads (including, for reasons discussed below, road-mobile ICBMs). Making progress could be challenging. Loading missiles with multiple warheads offers cost savings that are particularly attractive to Russia. Moreover, Russia has recently invested in a multiple warhead mobile ICBM, SS-27 mod 2 (usually known by its Russian name, RS-24), which could have a service life of three decades or more. There would likely be strong domestic opposition to any agreement that forced it to eliminate or modify this system.

Basing modes and crisis stability

Today, the United States has a triad of delivery systems (SSBNs, fixed ICBMs and bombers); Russia has a fourth in its road-mobile ICBMs. There is a widely held assumption that, to reduce costs, Russia and the US would eliminate some of these were they to make deep reductions.[23] If they did so, it seems most likely that they would move to a dyad. In this case, one option might be to retain both silo-based ICBMs and a mobile missile system (whether land or sea based).[24] The absence of a bomber force would, however, seriously curtail signalling options in a crisis. (Because the mobilisation of a bomber force would be very visible, it provides a convenient way of demonstrating resolve through the willingness to escalate.) A second option, therefore, would be to retain the bomber force and keep just one type of ballistic missile. From the perspective of crisis stability, if Russia or the US were to retain just one type of ballistic missile within a dyad, should it be a fixed or mobile system? (In the unlikely event that Russia and the US were to move to a 'monad', as the United Kingdom has done, this question would also be very salient.[25])

Both sea-launched and land-based missiles are more survivable – and so are often argued to be more stabilising – than silo-based ICBMs. In particular, Russia sees its mobile ICBMs as the most survivable of its four basing modes. However, much of this advantage derives from the fact that Russia's silo-based ICBMs are loaded with multiple warheads. If these missiles contained just one warhead each, the survivability advantages of mobile ICBMs would be considerably less marked (because it takes more than one warhead to reliably destroy a silo). Nevertheless, at low numbers, mobile delivery systems probably do retain a survivability edge for two reasons. Silo-based ICBMs are more vulnerable to cheating. If American and Russian silo-based ICBMs contained a single warhead and their total forces were equal in size, there would be little incentive for either side to pre-empt. However, if one side were to rapidly increase the number of warheads capable of hitting enemy silos – presumably in contravention of an arms-control agreement – stability might be undermined. At high numbers, cheating on a significant scale would be slow, costly and quickly detectable. As numbers come down, however, it might become more imaginable, particularly if Russia or the US were able to increase their forces without going to the trouble or expense of building more ICBMs by, for example, converting conventionally armed cruise missiles into nuclear-armed weapons. In contrast, because SSBNs and mobile ICBMs are generally targeted with conventional weapons, their survivability would be much less compromised by an opponent's cheating.

The survivability of mobile delivery systems is less likely to be compromised by technological change. Both Russia and the United States have long worried that technological breakthroughs might severely and suddenly undermine the survivability of their nuclear forces. No such breakthrough has occurred since the advent of the ballistic missile and the threat it posed to bomber bases. Whether such a breakthrough is likely to occur in future is extremely hard to predict, but if the aim is to ensure stability at low numbers for (potentially) many decades, this possibility cannot be ignored. In this regard, silo-based missiles appear to be the most vulnerable. This is not to downplay the very real difficulties of developing, say, high-precision conventional weapons that can reliably hold ICBM silos at risk. However, these difficulties seem less severe than the challenge facing the US in attempting to destroy dispersed Russian mobile ICBMs, or the challenge facing Russia in attempting to destroy the American SSBN force.

Other attributes of mobile missiles are, however, less desirable from the perspective of crisis stability. Russian land-based ICBMs are normally kept in 'pens' where they would be relatively vulnerable; only when dispersed are they highly survivable. The need to disperse mobile missiles in a crisis negatively impacts stability for two main reasons.[26] Firstly, a Russian leader might disperse these forces out of prudence but, in the process, send signals that had the unintended effect of escalating the crisis. (This is not to argue that leaders should not have signalling options at their disposal, but that it is undesirable if they are forced to signal in order to protect their forces). Secondly, the fear that Russia may disperse its forces could, perhaps, increase pressure on a US leader to attack them early in a crisis before they could be dispersed, using conventional weapons under the assumption that doing so would not trigger a nuclear reprisal.

These potentially dangerous dynamics might be exacerbated by deep reductions. Specifically, if Russia's mobile missiles were to make up a larger fraction of its total force at low numbers then there would be greater benefit to the US of destroying them and a corresponding greater incentive on Russia to disperse them earlier in a crisis 'just to be safe'.[27] If Russia's mobile missiles were loaded with multiple warheads this effect could be even more problematic, providing an important reason for eliminating all multiple-warhead missiles – even mobile ones – during the course of deep reductions.

It is also sometimes forgotten, particularly in the US, that SSBNs can have similar negative effects. Today, the US has 14 SSBNs of which four are at sea at any time. The remaining ten submarines, which are kept in port, are relatively vulnerable and, in a crisis, the US could send at least some of them to sea to protect them. Given the significant capability of the *Trident* D5 missile to destroy hardened targets, 'flushing' the submarine force would almost certainly spark Russian fears of a US first strike, regardless of whether that was the intention. (Some Russians worry particularly about a US strike on leadership launched from submarines close enough to the coast that there would be almost no warning.)[28] Again, if SSBNs were a larger fraction of the US force at lower numbers, a US leader might be pressured to flush the SSBN force earlier in a crisis, exacerbating instability.

On balance, because they are more survivable, mobile delivery vehicles probably do have a net advantage over single-warhead silo-based missiles at low numbers – but this is clearly an issue that would benefit from further study. That said, in the final analysis, history, domestic politics and culture may be at least as important as strategy in determining Russian and American choices about basing modes at low numbers. For instance, in the US, any suggestion that ICBMs should be scrapped meets with stringent opposition from Senators with missiles stationed in their states.[29] The Russian force posture would probably be

strongly influenced by its own distinctive domestic considerations. For these reasons, the postures adopted by Russia and
US at low numbers may well not be 'strategically optimal'. It
would, therefore, be important to recognise the stability challenges created by whatever force posture is chosen and develop
appropriate confidence-building measures.

CHAPTER FOUR

Rearmament stability

Russia and the United States might decide to make deep reductions in their nuclear arsenals, but they will not – indeed, they cannot – abandon the ability to rebuild them. Rearmament would be likely to undo any non-proliferation gains that Russia, and especially the United States, hope to obtain by working towards a world without nuclear weapons. Indeed, if rearmament were likely then there would be very little point in making deep reductions in the first place. Assessing the likelihood of rearmament is therefore an important part of the broader task of assessing the desirability of deep reductions.

Rearmament could occur on two different timescales. If, during the reductions process, warheads and delivery systems were mothballed but not destroyed, they could potentially be put back into service quickly. To avoid this possibility, it is assumed here that the series of agreements that facilitate deep reductions would, like most of their predecessors, mandate the actual destruction (or possibly the conversion) of key treaty-limited items.[1] In this case, rearmament could still occur – but only more slowly – because warheads and delivery systems would have to be remanufactured.

Except for cheating, the possibility of rearmament has not elicited all that much concern.[2] However, cheating is not the only – or probably even the most likely – form of rearmament. Although compliance concerns with US–Russian arms control agreements were sometimes raised, neither Russia (or the USSR) nor the United States ever accused the other of violating treaty-imposed 'central limits' on offensive strategic weapons. Looking forward, rearmament without violating treaty commitments – by waiting for treaties to expire or simply by abrogating them – is perhaps more likely. There can never be a guarantee that states will agree on a new arms-control agreement upon the expiration of an old one. From the expiration of the Strategic Arms Limitation Talks I Interim Agreement in 1977 to the entry into force of the Intermediate Nuclear Forces Treaty in 1988, there were no legally binding restraints on offensive nuclear arms. During this interregnum, both Russia and the United States augmented their deployed strategic nuclear forces. Legal rearmament through treaty abrogation is also possible. Neither power has ever withdrawn from a treaty related to strategic offensive weapons, but the US did withdraw from the Anti-Ballistic Missile Treaty in 2002 as well as the unratified but politically binding Strategic Arms Limitation Treaty (SALT) II agreement in 1986.

The problem of rearmament stability is not one that is purely associated with low numbers. Most nuclear-armed states, even though they have small arsenals, did not engage in arms racing. Conversely, as shown in Figure 2 (in the Appendix), the very high numbers of nuclear weapons acquired by the United States and the USSR did not prevent arms racing.

Armament drivers during the Cold War

One important driver of armament during the Cold War, particularly in the US, was military doctrine. From its very beginnings, US declaratory policy generally (but not exclusively) stated that the purpose of nuclear weapons was deterrence by punishment. In contrast, had deterrence failed, the early Cold War operational plans that have been declassified called for nuclear weapons to be used in much more traditional 'war-fighting' roles than inflicting punishment.[3] Defeating an enemy on the battlefield by using tactical nuclear weapons is an example of war-fighting; damage limitation is another. War-fighting, if planned for the purpose of deterrence rather than defeating an enemy once a war is under way, is an example of deterrence by denial.

A war-fighting doctrine emerged in the US right at the start of the Cold War. As early as April 1947, a key Air Force study argued that the atomic bomb was 'a strategic weapon to be expended only when and where its destructive force will contribute most toward the defeat of the enemy'.[4] This concept was embodied in war plans of the late 1940s and very early 1950s, which targeted cities, not in an effort to deter aggression by punishing it, but because hitting cities was believed to be the most effective way to defeat the Soviet Union.[5] Subsequent war plans contained strong elements of war-fighting, including nuclear attacks on Soviet conventional forces (known as retardation attacks).[6] These were intended to deny the Soviet Union its war aims in a European conflict and were included in war planning long before such attacks were advocated as a punishment strategy in the late 1970s.

A strategy of war-fighting encouraged high armament levels in the early Cold War for two reasons. Firstly, since the goal was military victory, the US target set (which included nuclear and conventional forces as well as infrastructure) was much larger than it would have been if the aim had just been punishment. Secondly, as an inevitable consequence of a war-fighting strategy, the size of the US force was dictated by the size of Soviet forces. As the Soviet Union built more airfields, launchers and delivery systems, the United States acquired and deployed more weapons in response.[7] In his seminal history of US nuclear war plans from 1945 to 1960, historian David Alan Rosenberg observes that 'US forces were routinely sized toward the objective of neutralizing Soviet nuclear forces' and, significantly, that during the late 1950s, 'expansion of the target list was largely attributable to identification of additional "counterforce" targets, in particular airfields and suspected missile sites'.[8] This expansion was accelerated by the military's interest in finding more targets to justify both existing weapons and requests for more.[9]

The dynamics became more complex during the Kennedy administration, which ultimately procured about double the number of *Polaris* submarines and *Minuteman* missiles programmed by the previous administration (while curtailing or eliminating other programmes). The military continued to agitate for more weapons on the basis of growing targeting requirements and this, along with a range of other considerations, led to the decision to develop MIRV technology, which ultimately facilitated a significant increase in warhead numbers in the 1970s.[10] However, political and bureaucratic factors became increasingly important. Historian Desmond Ball has argued that the Kennedy administration's procurement decisions were largely the result of bureaucratic bargaining and the political decision to stimulate the economy through military spending.[11] This process resulted in force levels higher than many key decision-makers felt was strategically necessary, but lower than the military wanted.

Bureaucratic politics appear to have been the key driver of Soviet armament. The Soviet Union had a war-fighting doctrine that was similar but not identical to the American one from the early Cold War. After Khrushchev's short-lived interest in a second-best strategic posture in the early 1960s, Soviet doctrine set the stage for a rapid expansion in warhead numbers. However, from the mid-1960s to the mid-1980s, the build-up was supply driven. The defence-industrial sector, with almost no oversight from either military or civilian leadership, 'used its political clout to deliver more weapons than the armed services asked for and even to build new weapon systems that the operational military did not want'.[12]

What might prompt a state to be the first to rearm?

Bureaucratic politics, domestic politics and the ever growing target lists created by a war-fighting doctrine all help explain the low level of armament stability during the first half of the Cold War. In the context of low numbers, domestic politics could, on balance, increase armament stability slightly compared to the Cold War. While the American public's fear of communism did not directly cause the US to produce over 70,000 nuclear weapons, it did make taxpayers more willing to accept the spending required for this build-up. Of course, if international relations worsen in future, populations could again become supportive of rearmament. It is entirely possible that, in such circumstances, nationalist politicians might adopt nuclear rearmament as a populist cause. On balance, however, deep reductions would probably be associated with nuclear weapons losing some of their salience and so taxpayers in democracies might become more reluctant to fund rearmament, but the effect is unlikely to be very significant.

Bureaucratic drivers of rearmament, which are generally peculiar to each state (and perhaps assume greater relative importance in countries under autocratic rule), would not seem, on average, to be any more or less important at low numbers than they have been in the past. Industrial considerations might, of course, be a significant barrier to reaching low numbers.

However, once defence contractors have oriented themselves away from nuclear weapons (as indeed many already have) they would be unlikely to agitate for rearmament.

In contrast, a war-fighting doctrine might make rearmament more likely at low numbers. A military guided by war-fighting plans could call for rearmament if an adversary began building forces or military infrastructure that it desired to hold at risk but could not do so without more nuclear weapons. Many nuclear-armed states, including those in NATO during the Cold War and Pakistan today, have used nuclear weapons to compensate for conventional inferiority. Based on this experience, the most likely trigger for nuclear rearmament might be the appearance of a growing conventional imbalance (although a build-up of biological or chemical weapons is another possibility). In fact, given that the conventional balance can be very hard to 'measure', especially if two sides have qualitatively different forces, the suspicion of a growing imbalance, based on factors that are hard to establish objectively, might be enough to spark rearmament. The key point is that a state with nuclear plenty could mount a nuclear response to a growing conventional imbalance by changing its war plans; a state with a small arsenal might decide that it must rearm to take on a new mission. Thus, nuclear rearmament to counter a growing conventional imbalance is an instability that could be a direct consequence of deep reductions.

In practice, stability could depend on how and whether mechanisms to address and stabilise conventional imbalances were implemented on the way to low numbers. Russia will probably not agree to deep reductions until progress is made in addressing its long-term concerns about both NATO and Chinese conventional forces. The US–China balance, particularly in the West Pacific, may also require attention. Even if China–Russia–US balances are handled adeptly, it is always possible that unforeseen conventional imbalances involving Russia or the United States could arise and prompt rearmament. If a phase of low numbers is to last many years (perhaps indefinitely), stability would be enhanced by Russia and the US moving away from war-fighting nuclear doctrines if they have not done so already. A state planning for deterrence by punishment would be less likely to respond to a growing conventional imbalance by building more nuclear weapons (although the possibility that it might do so anyway to satisfy domestic political concerns cannot be ruled out).

Other drivers of rearmament that were not so important during the Cold War could become significant at low numbers. As mentioned above, both the United States and Russia fear that technological developments could leave their arsenals vulnerable. If this were to transpire, rearmament would be one possible response. While such concerns would have to be significantly ameliorated for Russia in particular to agree to deep reductions, managing technological developments that had implications for nuclear force survivability could become an ongoing concern.

It is, however, the fear of nuclear compellence (that is, being on the receiving end of nuclear threats designed to force a state to do something it does not want to) that seems to underlie concerns about cheating at low numbers. This fear appears to be particularly acute in Russia, where some worry that China might attempt to use nuclear threats to acquire territory in Russia's Far East if it were ever to reach nuclear parity with Russia, let alone attain superiority.[13] Concerns about nuclear compellence stem from the intuitive argument that, in the past, when Russia and the US possessed thousands of warheads, nuclear imbalances on the order of hundreds of warheads posed little military significance. At low numbers, however, imbalances of the same size might be of much greater significance and facilitate successful compellence.[14] The desire to extract gains through nuclear compellence could, therefore, become a significant new motive for rearmament at low numbers.

Yet, these fears may be exaggerated. They stem, in part, from the belief that compellent threats have been effective in the past. In particular, US nuclear threats in 1953 are often seen as having been successful in compelling an end to the Korean War and are regarded as the key demonstration that compellence can 'work'.[15] However, the overwhelming majority of recent scholarship (much of it based on newly available historical documents) suggests that nuclear threats actually played a relatively modest role, if not an entirely negligible one.[16] There is scant evidence of successful compellence in other cases, including, for instance, the 1969 Madman Alert, in which US forces were placed on an increased state of alert (as part of a ploy on the part of President Richard Nixon to make the Soviet Union believe he was unstable and capable of doing anything to end the Vietnam War).[17] Moreover, even believers in the efficacy of nuclear compellence have to concede that it 'can work when it is credible, but it is likely to be credible only when the coercer enjoys superiority so great that it need not fear retaliation in kind'.[18] Assuming that Russia and the United States maintain highly survivable forces then, according to this logic, compellence would probably be ineffective at low numbers even if there were significant imbalances in force levels. It is also worth noting that building nuclear weapons for the specific purpose of compellence would appear to be historically unprecedented. While states have certainly made nuclear threats in the past to try to compel an adversary, and two nuclear weapons have even be used for that purpose, there does not seem to be any occasion on which a state built nuclear weapons specifically for compellence.

Nevertheless, such arguments may not convince those responsible for national security in Russia and the United

States that they need not worry about compellence (by each other or by a third state such as China). They could argue – and it would be difficult to disprove their case – that attempts at compellence might become more likely at low numbers because nuclear superiority would be more easily attainable. (It is much easier to build enough weapons to have double an opponent's arsenal if each side starts with 500 weapons, rather than 5,000).

A state considering rearmament with this logic in mind would, however, probably be deterred from the attempt if it believed that potential adversaries would also rearm because it would then be denied the numerical lead in nuclear weapons that it was seeking.[19] There is, therefore, a possible arms-control approach to managing concerns about compellence. If states' nuclear-weapons complexes were sufficiently transparent that no state could rearm without alerting others, there would be a significant deterrent to doing so. The challenges of designing and implementing such a verification scheme are considerable. Nuclear-weapons complexes would have to be limited in their production capacity, so that states could not rearm so quickly that others could not respond in time. The challenge of detecting clandestine nuclear-weapons production facilities would also arise. Finally, the political and technical challenges of facilitating inspections in highly sensitive facilities are considerable. Nevertheless, the fact that senior officials from some of the US National Laboratories are already thinking about the problem suggests it is worthy of serious consideration.[20]

If one state rearms, will the other follow?

If one state rearms, an adversary might do likewise – a process that could be termed 'responsive rearmament'. There would be at least four strategic rationales for responsive rearmament. Firstly, a state watching another rearm might fear for the survivability of its nuclear forces and build more to compensate (it might even rearm out of a mistaken belief that an adversary was rearming). Secondly, in a state with a war-fighting doctrine, the logic of war planning might demand rearmament (because the size of a nuclear force needed for war-fighting is very dependent upon the size of an adversary's force). Thirdly, fearing that it could become the victim of nuclear compellence, a state might rearm to restore parity. Lastly, a state with extended deterrence commitments might rearm to reassure its allies.

The likelihood of responsive rearmament would probably depend, in considerable measure, on a state's doctrine and posture. A war-fighting doctrine would be more likely to precipitate responsive rearmament than a 'deterrence by punishment' one. A state would be less likely to undertake responsive rearmament if its principal delivery systems were mobile (land- or sea-based), since these are much less vulnerable to nuclear attack than silo-based ICBMs. Survivable forces such as these might also ease fears of nuclear compellence.

That said, such strategic considerations would not be the only – perhaps not even the main – potential drivers of responsive rearmament. Politics – domestic and international – could also be very important, especially if rearmament were in violation of an agreement. Even though a militarily significant violation at low numbers might be, say, tens of weapons, one analyst has noted that 'politically, the deployment of one "extra" ICBM would be significant, raising doubts about purposes, intentions, trust etc.'.[21] While it might be more realistic to say that the deployment of one extra weapon could be significant, depending on the politics of the moment, militarily insignificant violations can have significant political ramifications.

The Soviet placement of medium- and intermediate-range ballistic missiles in Cuba in 1962 is the most famous example of a clearly definable incident of 'responsive armament' (since the Soviet Union was still building up this was not rearmament). The lead-up to the Cuban Missile Crisis created pressures in the Soviet Union that were, perhaps, similar to those that might be generated if Russia or the US were to discover that the other had started to rearm.

In March 1962, as noted above, Khrushchev was informed that the United States had planned for a first strike the previous summer and this sparked fears of becoming the victim of compellence; fears exacerbated by the poor survivability of the Soviet arsenal. The following month, Khrushchev was apparently deeply affected by a briefing in which he was informed that it would take ten years to achieve parity in ICBMs with the United States.[22] Placing missiles in Cuba appears, in part, to have been a response to this revelation.[23] Historians Richard Ned Lebow and Janice Gross Stein have also stressed the role of Soviet domestic politics, arguing that failing reforms had left Khrushchev vulnerable to 'mounting pressure from militants to display uncompromising toughness to the capitalist world'.[24] Khrushchev's actions, therefore, appear to have been influenced by most, if not all, of the factors identified above as potential drivers of responsive rearmament.

Nuclear multipolarity

During the Cold War, deterrence was characterised by bipolarity. The arsenals of smaller nuclear-armed states did not then seem – nor do they now, retrospectively – to have much influence on the central US–Soviet confrontation. Although the US and the USSR did plan for nuclear contingencies involving other nuclear-armed states, each was very much the focus of the other's planning. Meanwhile, deterrence theorists concentrated almost exclusively on the case of bipolar nuclear confrontations.[1] When this focus was explained, which it rarely was, it was argued that the British, Chinese, French, and Israeli arsenals could be ignored because they were so much smaller than those of Russia and the US. Out of this line of thought emerges the concern that if Russia and the United States were to make deep reductions, the arsenals of other nuclear-armed states would increase in relative importance and deterrence would become more multipolar.[2] (The term 'polarity' is used here, as elsewhere in the deterrence literature, to describe the structure of deterrence relations; it is not used in its more common political science sense to describe the broader distribution of power in the international system). However, it is really the size of the American and Russian arsenals that is responsible today – and was responsible in the Cold War – for the absence of deterrence multipolarity?

Alliances

A multipolar world in which all the deterrence dyads operated completely independently of one another would probably not be much more unstable than a bipolar one.[3] However, in most situations it would be very unlikely for the deterrence dyads to operate independently of one another. In particular, it is possible for nuclear-armed states to form alliances, in which they pool their nuclear arsenals (and other 'strategic assets' such as high-precision conventional munitions and ballistic-missile defence systems). Thus states must worry about deterring not just other states but also hostile alliances.[4] ('Alliance', in this context, refers solely to a bloc in which nuclear-armed states plan joint nuclear operations; other types of security alliances do not create the same problems for strategic stability.) In theory, this might become increasingly problematic as numbers come down. Analysing deep reductions during the Cold War, James N. Miller (now US principal deputy under secretary of defense for policy) argued that 'if China, France, Great Britain, the Soviet Union, and the United States each had 50 nuclear warheads, each country would face a potential coalition of 200 bombs to its 50'.[5]

The possibility of alliance formation – formally or in effect – can create serious instabilities. If states require the ability to be able to retaliate, by themselves, against any possible coalition, they could engage in frantic arms racing. Even states in alliances might feel the need to do so out of the fear of abandonment. In the worst case, a state that lagged behind might find itself in a position of overwhelming strategic inferiority relative to some newly formed hostile alliance, creating dangerous crisis instabilities. In this way, multipolarity can exacerbate both crisis and arms race instability. The result might be termed 'alliance instability'. Such instability – a potential result of multipolarity – is undesirable. The question here is whether deep reductions would generate it.

The size of the American and Soviet arsenals is, at best, only a partial explanation for the absence of alliance instability during the Cold War. While these arsenals may have inoculated the US and the USSR against the possibility of hostile alliance formation, China, France and the UK enjoyed no such protection.

The idea that the US and the USSR might team up to launch a joint first strike on China was far from purely hypothetical. In May 1963 and again in September 1964, in the run up to China's first nuclear test, the US floated the idea with the USSR but was rebuffed.[6] The tables were turned in 1969 when the Soviet Union, at the height of the Sino-Soviet border crisis, attempted to gauge US reaction to a Soviet strike on China and was met with a stern warning not to act. When approached about participating in, or at least condoning, a first strike on China, each superpower demurred, seeing a nuclear-armed China as a useful counterbalance to the other's power. President Nixon reflected this when he 'startled his cabinet colleagues' in 1969 by arguing that 'it was against our interests to let China be "smashed" in some Sino-Soviet war'.[7] The Soviet Union presumably felt similarly about a Sino-American war in 1963–64.

In short, China was not affected by alliance instabilities – even though it had a small arsenal – because it was politically impossible for the US and the USSR to form even a temporary alliance against it. Chinese nuclear doctrine also helped. Had it followed US or Russian theories of deterrence, China would have built up its arsenal frantically in order to deter either, let alone both of them together. Instead, it remained content with just a few hundred nuclear weapons.

Alliance instability could also have been a problem for France and the United Kingdom. It is possible to imagine either choosing to build much larger forces than they did out of fear that they would be abandoned by the United States and become the victim of a Soviet first strike. Two factors explain their decisions not to. Firstly, both adopted doctrines that emphasised the value of small nuclear forces (doctrines that were, at least in part, developed to justify the small arsenals that they could afford). Secondly, the strength of the NATO alliance probably also acted as a break on the size of their arsenals, although much more so in the case of the UK than France. The size of the US arsenal was at most a secondary factor in ensuring the success of NATO. Fundamentally, the alliance's strength derived from shared values, interests and threats. Importantly, the Soviet Union saw NATO in a similar way. It assumed that, in a deep crisis, the three Western allies would stand together.[8] Whether this assumption was correct (and, from a NATO perspective, it sometimes felt questionable) is beside the point; that the Soviet Union believed it helped deter Soviet attacks against France and the UK. Again, it was politics, not arsenal size, that ensured a high degree of alliance stability where France and the UK were concerned.

There is, however, one way in which high numbers may have prevented alliance instability during the Cold War: by reducing Soviet concerns about the possibility of a joint first strike by the three nuclear-armed NATO states. As numbers come down, the significance of the existing alliance between France, the UK and the US is likely to increase. Even during START I negotiations, UK–US nuclear weapons cooperation was a concern for the USSR. The end of the Cold War may have removed this concern for now, but it is likely to re-emerge as deep reductions are contemplated – as Lavrov emphasised in 2010.[9] British and French involvement in some form of multilateral arms control process could potentially ease these concerns.

Two points emerge from this discussion. Firstly, alliance instability is primarily a potential consequence of shifting alliances. After the Sino-Soviet split, Cold War alliances were relatively static; alliances were either impossible (in the case of China, the US and the USSR) or reasonably strong and constant (in the case of NATO). Secondly, the pattern of alliances was, at root, a result of Cold War politics. Balance-of-power considerations prevented even temporary alliances in the Chinese–Soviet–US strategic triangle; shared interests sustained NATO. The size of the American and Soviet arsenals hardly mattered. This suggests that deep reductions would not, by themselves, lead to alliance instability. The only exception relates to the one existing alliance between the three nuclear-armed NATO states, and here some form of arms control might be required to prevent instability with Russia.

This same conclusion is borne out by the South Asian experience. In theory, China and Pakistan could launch a joint first strike on India. The steps that India might take to counter such as threat, such as rapidly expanding its arsenal, could exacerbate the ongoing competition in fissile-material production between India and Pakistan. Fortunately, Indian military planners do not worry about this eventuality and it does not guide their planning.[10] Arsenal size does play some part in moderating Indian threat perceptions. Because China's arsenal is considerably larger and more capable than Pakistan's, Indian planners feel that if they can deter China they can also deter a joint attack. Importantly, they also judge that, in spite of China's close relations with Pakistan (which included aid to Pakistan's nuclear-weapons programme), Sino-Pakistani joint nuclear weapons planning is extremely unlikely. Once again, it is the political infeasibility of alliance formation – not numbers – that is primarily responsible for preventing instability.

None of this is to say that alliance instabilities will not arise in future. They might, especially if proliferation occurs and nuclear-armed states start entering and leaving alliances more freely and frequently than in the past. It is possible to disagree about whether this is likely. However, it was not arsenal size that prevented this kind of instability during the Cold War – nor does it prevent it today – and it is, therefore, unlikely that deep reductions by Russia and the United States would trigger the fundamental readjustment of alliance politics that would be required to cause instability.

Opportunism

Another theoretical difference between a bipolar and a multipolar world is the possibility that a third state could take opportunistic advantage of a conflict between two other countries. Nuclear opportunism does not seem to have attracted much attention in the academic literature, but it is a concern of military planners.[11] For instance, while Indian military planners do not worry about a joint Sino-Pakistani first strike, they definitely worry about the possibility that if India and China went to war, Pakistan could attack India opportunistically (not by prior arrangement with China) in order to settle old scores over Kashmir.[12] A two-front war such as this, in which three-way nuclear signalling would be possible, could exhibit a very low degree of crisis stability.

US allies express similar fears. For instance, in an interview one former Japanese official stated that his principal fear about deep reductions was that if the United States were caught up in a nuclear contingency in the Middle East, it might not have nuclear weapons to spare to deal with a simultaneous conflict in East Asia (his implication being that China might use a Middle

Eastern war in which the US was involved as an opportunity to initiate a conflict with Japan).[13]

Numbers have some bearing on the potential for opportunism because, as arsenals shrink, states would probably plan to use a larger fraction of their available weapons in the event of a nuclear war, leaving less in reserve to deter opportunism. However, survivability is probably more important than arsenal size per se. For instance, if the US ever came close to attaining an effective first strike against Russia then, in the event of all-out nuclear war in which the US struck first, Russia would be left vulnerable to opportunism. Thus, opportunism could be a problem at 500 warheads, if Russia or the US had just enough nuclear weapons after absorbing a first strike to deter the other, but no more. Whether opportunism would be a problem can really only be answered by Russia and the US themselves with knowledge of their deterrence requirements and projected force postures and capabilities. However, it would be easier for Russia and the United States to be confident of the sufficiency of their reserves if they were also confident in the sizes and capabilities of all other states' arsenals (and if these were appropriately constrained). This constitutes another important strategic reason for bringing China, France and the UK into the arms-control process before Russia and the US reach their level.

China's 'sprint to parity' and proliferation

One of the most commonly expressed fears about deep US–Russian reductions is that they might 'lower the cost of entry to peer status' and prompt China (and possibly even India and Pakistan) to build up their nuclear arsenals quickly in an attempt to 'sprint to parity'.[14] A related fear is that non-nuclear-weapon states might, for similar reasons, decide to acquire small nuclear arsenals.[15] Whether deep reductions would encourage a Chinese sprint to parity or spur proliferation is an open question. It is also somewhat beside the point because an arms-control regime can, should and in practice would be designed to make these possibilities unlikely to materialise and to mitigate their consequences if they do.[16]

Fears of proliferation are misplaced because current bilateral US–Russian arms reductions will not continue indefinitely, and China, France and the UK will not join the process, unless non-nuclear-weapon states agree to strengthen the non-proliferation regime. Indeed, as described in the introduction, the desire to create a disarmament-for-nonproliferation quid pro quo was largely responsible for motivating the nuclear-weapon states' current interest in disarmament. There has been much argument about whether this policy is likely to succeed. However, if it fails, Russia and the US are unlikely to reduce their arsenals to a point that may encourage proliferation. Moreover, if all states were collectively committed to disarmament, future proliferators would be much more likely than they are today to be confronted by a unified coalition of nuclear-armed states determined to prevent them from succeeding.

A Chinese sprint to parity could probably be deterred by Russia and the United States maintaining a visible reconstitution capability that would allow them to respond in kind to a sudden Chinese build-up. Indeed, this concept was endorsed by the 2010 Nuclear Posture Review in the form of a 'revitalized infrastructure'.[17] Yet, even this sensible step is unlikely to prove necessary because, for reasons of domestic politics, Russia and the US will not reduce their arsenals to the point where China might attempt a sprint to parity, unless they receive credible assurances from China that it would not do so. Even during New START negotiations, there was some relatively muted criticism in the US that the process did not include China.[18] As the American and Russian arsenals shrink, this criticism will grow. Initially, greater transparency about China's capabilities and plans might be sufficient to assuage American and Russian concerns. However, before reaching parity with China, Russia and the US will inevitably insist upon Chinese involvement in formal multilateral arms reductions (which would probably necessitate involving France and the UK too).[19]

It is by no means certain that China (let alone or India or Pakistan at some later stage) will be willing to take part in multilateral nuclear-arms reductions, or even to be more transparent; it is only a prediction that China's failure to participate would impose a floor on US–Russia reductions, thus precluding the possibility of a Chinese sprint to parity in the first place. There does appear, however, to be growing internal debate within China about the conditions under which it would take part in multilateral arms-limitation talks, and there are at least some who are sympathetic to the idea of accepting a treaty that mandates unequal arsenal sizes in return for concrete actions from the US to demonstrate that it has accepted mutual vulnerability.[20]

CONCLUSIONS

Nuclear deterrence is often treated by Russia and the United States as a numbers game. They generally assume that, during the Cold War, large arsenals bolstered deterrence and enhanced stability (in part by preventing multipolarity). Deep reductions are seen as a step into the unknown. On the contrary, however, experience from the Cold War when one or both superpowers had small arsenals, as well as the experience of states that never built large arsenals, reveals much about deterrence at low numbers as well as a misreading of history.

Large arsenals contribute little to the effectiveness of deterrence, even extended deterrence. The success of extended deterrence in the Cold War was the result of the strength of the US political commitment to its allies, not the size of its arsenal. Looking forward, there can be no guarantee that deterrence will always work (at high or low numbers). If the US loses conventional dominance in key regions, security commitments to allies may lack credibility. Large nuclear arsenals would, however, not provide an antidote.

Strategic stability at low numbers might be somewhat more problematic. Rearmament in the face of a growing conventional imbalance is a potentially a serious problem. Likewise, reductions could exacerbate Russian fears about the survivability of its arsenal and undermine crisis stability. But big arsenals are no panacea. They did not prevent a Cold War arms race. Nor do they preclude the possibility for crisis instabilities between Russia and the United States. Indeed, the potential for instability today provides the strongest reason for arms control – that enhanced stability would enable a move to lower numbers is an added benefit.

The size of the American and Soviet arsenals in the Cold War cannot really explain the absence of multipolarity. Fundamentally, its absence was the result of alliance structures being relatively static. These structures were dictated by shared interests and balance-of-power politics, not arsenal size. If in future alliances become more fluid than in the past, deterrence might well become more multipolar and unstable. However, deep US–Russian reductions would be unlikely to effect such a change – with the one important exception that they would exacerbate Russian fears of joint nuclear action by the existing alliance of France, the UK and the US.

The prospects for deterrence at low numbers are, therefore, generally good. However, some arms-control measures would be required on the way down to ensure stability – and these could prove rather challenging to negotiate and implement.[1]

The first step is for Russia and the United States to build on New START and negotiate towards a more wide-ranging agreement that covers all nuclear weapons (strategic, tactical, deployed and non-deployed) and puts them back on the path of eliminating missiles capable of carrying multiple warheads.[2] Although such an agreement poses severe verification and definitional challenges, a greater difficulty – at this and probably subsequent stages of the reductions process – will be easing Russian fears over ballistic-missile defence and high-precision conventional weapons. Even optimistic observers believe it is very unlikely that the next bilateral arms-control agreement will mandate reductions to anywhere near the level of 1,000 warheads of all types; 2,000 to 3,000 warheads seems a more likely figure. If this prediction is correct then further stages of bilateral arms control would be appropriate. At some point in the process, Russia and the US will need to develop transparency arrangements for their nuclear-weapons production complexes so that each is confident that it would receive timely warning of rearmament by the other.

At some yet-to-be-determined point in the reductions process – but significantly before Russia and United States reach parity with any other state – Moscow and Washington are likely to refuse to make further reductions unless they are reassured that China will not sprint to parity. Russia will also require reassurance that combined American, British and French nuclear forces could not launch a successful first strike. Today, France possesses fewer than 300 nuclear weapons. The United Kingdom certainly has fewer than France and China probably does too. If none of these states significantly increases the size of its arsenal then Russia and the United States may be willing to go to 500 warheads if China, France and the UK commit not to increase their stockpiles and take on verification provisions to make such a commitment credible.

China, however, is augmenting its nuclear forces, albeit very slowly. If it makes significant increases then Russia and the US are likely to demand its involvement in a very complicated and difficult multilateral reductions process. In the near term, greater transparency by China is a key first step towards reassuring Russia and the United States. China, however, is fearful of US intentions and uses opacity to enhance the survivability of its nuclear forces. A first-order task, therefore, is for the US and China to develop a dialogue that would allow each to reassure the other about its intentions – if, indeed, they are benign. One potential complicating factor in all of this is India and Pakistan. Today, each probably possesses fewer than 100 nuclear weapons but both are building more. If China builds up its arsenal in response to India then the complexity of facilitating deep reductions will be magnified yet further. Unfortunately, the prospects for a fissile material cut-off treaty, which would ban the production of fissile material for military purposes and hence cap the Indian and Pakistani build-ups, are currently bleak.

Conventional force balancing is another central challenge. To ensure rearmament stability at low numbers, it will be necessary to stabilise the balances between NATO and Russia, China and the US, and China and Russia. Of these, only the NATO–Russian balance has been subject to arms control in the past. However, the Conventional Forces in Europe Treaty, which regulated the conventional balance in Europe, lies in tatters following Russia's 'suspension' of its participation in the treaty in 2008.[3] The extent to which Russian concerns about conventional imbalances – with China and NATO – will affect its willingness to discuss tactical nuclear weapons in the next round of nuclear-arms negotiations is extremely hard to judge right now. What is clear is that at some point conventional imbalances will become a barrier to further reductions. Encouragingly, the Obama administration has put considerable effort into resuscitating the Conventional Forces in Europe Treaty – although it is still far from certain whether these efforts will succeed.[4]

These items, by themselves, present a challenging agenda. However, the biggest hurdles to reaching low numbers may not be strategic. Both Russia and the United States face their own distinctive political challenges. To develop a viable strategy for reaching low numbers it is first necessary to recognise these challenges.

Any discussion of the political hurdles to gaining Moscow's agreement to deep reductions is necessarily rather speculative. However, unlike in the United States, treaty ratification does not seem problematic. If Russian domestic politics remain anything like they are today, the Kremlin will probably not have too much trouble convincing the Federation Council and State Duma (the upper and lower houses of the Russian parliament) to ratify any treaty that it has negotiated. One challenge is that the Kremlin may not want to reduce its arsenal significantly because of the prestige it associates with nuclear weapons possession (the US also accords nuclear weapons prestige, although considerably less). Its strategic concerns about deep reductions can (in theory at least) be reduced by arms control. It may be harder to convince it that its status will not be irreparably damaged. Summarising the outlook of Russian leaders towards disarmament efforts, Moscow-based analyst Dmitri Trenin argues that

> even when and if it succeeds in its conventional modernization program, Russia's resources – financial, economic, and not least demographic – will prevent Moscow from claiming an equal military status with the United States and, in conventional terms, also with China. For this reason alone, Russian leaders will likely always see value in nuclear forces as defining Russia's claim to a seat at the table with the other world powers.[5]

The United States faces its own challenges. Alliance relations are one. Given that much effort will be needed to persuade allies that deep reductions would not undermine their security, the United States must engage with them and narrow the gap between what they believe is necessary for extended deterrence and what it believes is necessary. The Obama administration has already started on this process and developed new consultation mechanisms for non-NATO allies.[6] This process now needs to be further institutionalised and strengthened.

Of course, domestic politics pose another, perhaps greater challenge for the United States. There will always be a tendency for political opponents, particularly on the right, to accuse an administration concluding an arms-reduction agreement of being weak on national security. (In particular, it is always possible for critics to find ways in which a verification regime could be strengthened and use them as an argument against the treaty). During the New START ratification debate, for instance, would-be Republican presidential nominees and conservative lobbying groups vigorously opposed the treaty.[7] Yet, public opinion remained staunchly in favour of ratification. A CNN poll, for instance, placed public support at 73%.[8] In fact, over the last 50 years, the US public has generally been supportive of specific arms-control agreements and, in the absence of a major new security threat emerging, it is hard to see why this would change.[9] Public support for a treaty does not, however, translate into a guarantee of ratification. Arms control is not a key issue for most American voters and Senators are unlikely to lose much support by opposing an agreement.

In the final analysis, the greatest domestic challenge facing an administration – particularly a Democratic one – concluding an arms-control agreement is securing the Senate's support. Between 1963, when the Limited Test Ban Treaty was ratified during the Kennedy administration, and 2010, when New START was ratified, no nuclear arms-control treaty was 'cleanly' ratified under a Democratic president.[10] Even New START, modest though it was, proved challenging to ratify. The Senate may have been perfectly in line with public opinion (with 73% of the Senators present voting for ratification), but given that two-thirds of them were required for the Senate to provide its advice and consent, the margin of victory was actually a fairly narrow one. Securing the overwhelming support required for future treaties to be ratified is far from assured, especially given the sensitivity of the Senate to any perceived concessions on ballistic-missile defense and high-precision conventional weapons – two areas of vital interest to Moscow.

One important step will be for the US to revise its nuclear war plans. In part, this is needed simply because reductions necessitate further prioritisation in targeting. However, it is also politically important. An arms-control treaty cannot be ratified unless the uniformed military 'certifies' that the US will have enough nuclear weapons after reductions to meet its deterrence requirements. When the uniformed military makes statements about sufficiency they are generally not making a statement about an adversary's pain threshold but rather calculating whether they can continue to fulfill the requirements of extant war planning. Changing war plans can, therefore, help to create the political conditions necessary for deep reductions, but it is likely to prove a much harder task than it might first appear. Based on past experience, particularly during the 1994 Nuclear Posture Review, attempts to overhaul US nuclear war planning can generate tremendous bureaucratic opposition. Overcoming this opposition will require sustained attention from the highest levels of government.[11]

Perhaps the most fundamental political issue is whether the goal that motivates deep reductions – the pursuit of a world without nuclear weapons – actually undermines their prospects. The Obama administration believes it must be vocal on the international stage about the renewed American interest in disarmament if it is to achieve the non-proliferation benefits that it seeks. One by-product of this strategy, however, has been to reduce the attractiveness of deep reductions to those who are not ideologically opposed to cuts but are skeptical of the pursuit of abolition. Senator Johnny Isakson (Republican–Georgia), for instance, may have voted for New START, but he distanced himself from the administration when he stated that 'only through setting the example, without giving in or capitulating a thing, do we give hope to the future that my grandchildren and yours can live in a world that will not be free of nukes but will be secure'.[12]

Yet, the reality is that it is not necessary to decide now whether abolition is desirable or feasible. While deep reductions are certainly consistent with abolition, they would also not force the United States to eliminate its remaining weapons if the security conditions were not amenable. Thus, if deterrence at low numbers is unproblematic, as argued in this book, deep reductions could form the basis for a consensus on US nuclear policy that has been lacking since the end of the Cold War. Specifically, it might be possible to build support around cutting nuclear arsenals significantly and then reassessing the prospects for abolition from that 'vantage point'.[13] Indeed, this may be the de facto policy of the Obama administration. It was very noticeable that, during the New START ratification debate, the administration hardly talked about its long-term vision and instead tried to sell the treaty on its merits. It remains to be seen whether this strategy, which is also likely to be embraced by future administrations seeking ratification of arms-control agreements, will mollify domestic opposition.

Where are we now?

At their high-water marks, the Soviet and US nuclear arsenals numbered 45,000 (in 1986) and 32,000 (in 1966) respectively.[1] Today, 20 years after the end of the Cold War, Russia still possesses an estimated 12,000 warheads and the United States about 9,400.[2]

Some of the weapons in the Russian and US stockpiles have been retired but not yet dismantled. On 3 May 2010, the United States took the unprecedented step of revealing that the total size of its operational stockpile on 30 September 2009 was 5,113 warheads.[3] The remainder of its arsenal is awaiting dismantlement – a process that could take around a decade given that the US has recently dismantled an average of about 400 warheads per year. Russia has not officially revealed the size of its operational stockpile, but it is believed to be about 4,600 warheads.[4]

The Russian and US arsenals can be sub-divided into two basic categories: strategic and tactical, although the latter are also sometimes called non-strategic, sub-strategic, theatre, short-range or battlefield weapons. (Unfortunately, these terms are incorrectly used more-or-less interchangeably.) Tactical nuclear weapons were originally conceived as short-range low-

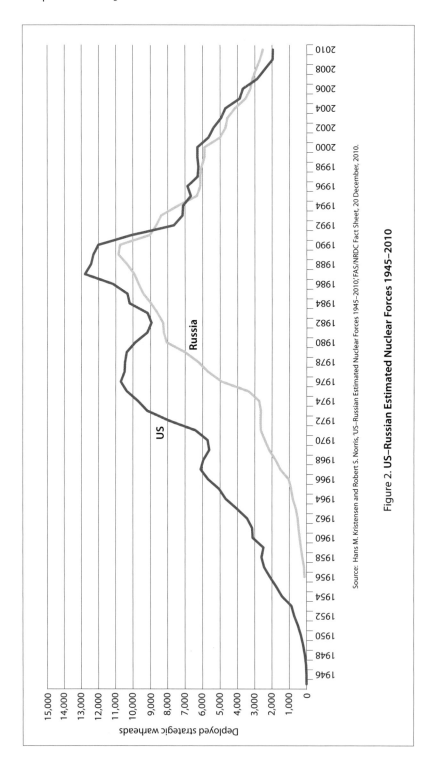

Figure 2. US–Russian Estimated Nuclear Forces 1945–2010

Source: Hans M. Kristensen and Robert S. Norris, 'US–Russian Estimated Nuclear Forces 1945–2010,' FAS/NRDC Fact Sheet, 20 December, 2010.

Table 2: **Russian and US strategic force structures**

	Russia		United States	
	Deployed DVs	Deployed warheads	Deployed DVs	Deployed warheads
Silo-based ICBMs	160	910	450	500
Road-mobile ICBMs	171	180	0	0
SLBMs	160	576	288	1,152
Bombers	75	838	60	316

DV=Delivery vehicle; ICBM=intercontinental ballistic missile; SLBM=sea-launched ballistic missile. Sources: Robert S. Norris and Hans M. Kristensen, 'Russian Nuclear Forces, 2010', *Bulletin of the Atomic Scientists*, vol. 66, no. 1, January–February 2010, p. 76; Robert S. Norris and Hans M. Kristensen, 'U.S. Nuclear Forces, 2010', *Bulletin of the Atomic Scientists*, vol. 66, no. 3, May–June 2010, p. 58.

yield weapons that could be used to gain tactical advantage during military operations. Today, the broad class labelled as tactical includes weapons for use on the battlefield, in anti-submarine warfare and for air defence. As a general rule, tactical and strategic weapons can be distinguished on the basis of their range. However, there are no hard and fast rules; the distinction has also been shaped by the weapons that Russia and the United States wanted to leave out of past strategic arms control negotiations. Nuclear-armed sea-launched cruise missiles, for instance, are anomalous. Modern sea-launched cruise missiles have ranges significantly in excess of early sea-launched ballistic missiles and are essentially equal in range to air-launched cruise missiles.[5] Yet, sea-launched ballistic missiles and air-launched cruise missiles are both considered strategic, whereas sea-launched cruise missiles are considered tactical. More fundamentally, distinguishing between tactical and strategic nuclear weapons is artificial because any use of a tactical nuclear weapon – even against an isolated military target with no civilian deaths – would inevitably be of profound strategic significance.

As shown in Figure 2, the total number of strategic warheads deployed by Russia and the United States continued to grow throughout the Cold War, peaking in the US at 13,685 (in 1987) and in the Soviet Union at 11,529 (in 1989).[6] Today, as a result of both arms control and unilateral decisions, the US deploys about 2,000 strategic warheads and Russia about 2,600.[7] New START will further limit each side, nominally to 1,550 deployed strategic warheads. However, since nuclear-capable bombers are counted as carrying one warhead (even though they can actually carry many more), the actual number of warheads deployed will be slightly higher.

Although Russia and the US have similarly sized stockpiles, there are some very significant differences in their composition. The United States has a triad of strategic delivery systems in its silo-based ICBMs, sea-launched ballistic missiles carried by SSBNs and heavy bombers capable of carrying air-launched cruise missiles or gravity bombs. In addition to these basing modes, Russia has road-mobile ICBMs. The differing Russian and US force structures are shown in Table 2.

Russia and the US load their ICBM forces in quite different ways. All American ICBMs and various classes of Russian ICBMs are capable of carrying multiple warheads. For reasons discussed above, a long-standing American goal of arms control was to eliminate all such ICBMs. This goal was accomplished by the administration of Bill Clinton in START II, but this agreement did not enter into force. The administration of George W. Bush, by contrast, rejected the concept of treaty-imposed limits on force structure and the arms-control treaty it negotiated, the 2002 Moscow Treaty, did not constrain multiple-warhead ICBMs. However, it decided to remove (or download) ICBM warheads anyway. By the time Bush left office in January 2009, the United States' 450 ICBMs were loaded just with 550 warheads out of the 1,350 they can carry.[8] This process was continued by the Obama administration, which has decided to load all US ICBMs with just one warhead. To achieve numerical parity with the US at lower costs, Russia loads its missiles with as many warheads as they will carry. Its 160 silo-based ICBMs are loaded with an average of 5.7 warheads each.[9] Although almost all of Russia's 170 or so mobile ICBMs currently contain a single warhead, its newest mobile missile, SS-27 mod. 2 (more usually referred to by its Russian name, RS-24), which was first deployed in 2010 and will probably be produced in large numbers, can be loaded with three or four.[10]

Another important difference between the American and Russian strategic arsenals is in their reserve forces. The United States has slightly fewer than 2,000 non-deployed strategic warheads in storage.[11] Given the many unused 'slots' on US delivery vehicles, some of these warheads could be redeployed relatively quickly.[12] This so-called upload potential is a matter of serious concern to Russia, which lacks an equivalent reserve. The operational lifetime of Russian warheads is reported to be only ten or 15 years.[13] This makes it challenging for Russia to maintain a large reserve stockpile.

The asymmetry between Russian and US nuclear forces extends to their tactical nuclear weapons – although here it is Russia that has the numerical advantage. By the end of the Cold War, each superpower had more tactical warheads than the total number it possess today. In 1987, for instance, the United States had about 10,000 nuclear warheads that were not considered strategic; the Soviet Union had well over twice that number.[14] That year, the Soviet Union and the United States signed the Intermediate Nuclear Forces Treaty, under which they eliminated many of their longer-range tactical systems, specifically all their nuclear-armed ground-launched ballistic and cruise missiles with ranges between 500km and 5,500km. Since then, through unverified unilateral actions, both sides have further reduced their tactical nuclear forces. The United States retains about 1,100–1,200 tactical gravity bombs (of which about 400 are deployed) along with 100 sea-launched cruise missiles, which it is committed to dismantling.[15] Russia has many more tactical nuclear weapons, although exactly how many is unclear. US analysts Robert S. Norris and Hans M. Kristensen estimate that Russia has about 2,000 operational tactical nuclear weapons and a further 3,400 or so in reserve or awaiting dismantlement.[16] These include warheads for gravity bombs, sea-launched cruise missiles, air defence and anti-missile systems, anti-submarine weapons, torpedoes and possibly short-range ballistic missiles.

GLOSSARY

ICBM	intercontinental ballistic missile
MIRV	multiple independent re-entry vehicle
SSBN	ballistic-missile submarine
SALT II	Strategic Arms Limitation Treaty II
START	Strategic Arms Reduction Treaty
TEL	Transporter-erector-launcher

Introduction

1   Remarks by President Barack Obama, Prague, 5 April 2009, http://www. whitehouse.gov/the_press_office/ Remarks-By-President-Barack-Obama-In-Prague-As-Delivered/.

2   Joint Statement by President Obama and President Medvedev, 1 April 2009, http://www.america.gov/st/texttrans-english/2009/April/20090401125216xjs nommiso.8078381.html.

3   For a discussion of those conditions see George Perkovich and James M. Acton, *Abolishing Nuclear Weapons*, Adelphi Paper 396 (Abingdon: Routledge for the IISS, 2008).

4   See, for example, Jon Kyl, 'The New Start Treaty: Time for a Careful Look', *Wall Street Journal*, 8 July 2010, http:// online.wsj.com/article/SB100014240527 4870429360457534336085010776o.html.

5   Lawrence Freedman, 'Nuclear Disarmament: From a Popular Movement to an Elite Project, and Back Again?', in George Perkovich and James M. Acton (eds), *Abolishing Nuclear Weapons: A Debate* (Washington, DC: Carnegie Endowment for International Peace, 2009), http:// www.carnegieendowment.org/files/

abolishing_nuclear_weapons_debate. pdf, pp. 144–47; Brad Roberts, 'On Order, Stability, and Nuclear Abolition', in Perkovich and Acton (eds), *Abolishing Nuclear Weapons: A Debate*, pp. 166–69; Keith Payne, 'How Much is Enough?: A Goal-Driven Approach to Defining Key Principles', Third Annual Conference on Strategic Weapons in the 21st Century, Washington DC, 29 January 2009, http:// www.lanl.gov/conferences/sw/2009/ docs/payne_livermore-2.pdf; Bruce Blair, Victor Esin, Matthew McKinzie, Valery Yarynich and Pavel Zolotarev, 'Smaller and Safer: A New Plan for Nuclear Postures', *Foreign Affairs*, vol. 89, no. 5, September–October 2010, pp. 9–16.

6   *Nuclear Posture Review Report* (US Department of Defense, 2010), http:// www.defense.gov/npr/docs/2010 nuclear posture review report.pdf, pp. 29–30.

7   Important previous academic work on this question includes Francis P. Hoeber, 'How Little is Enough?', *International Security*, vol. 3, no. 3, Winter 1978–1979, pp. 53–73; Michael

M. May, George F. Bing and John D. Steinbruner, 'Strategic Arsenals After START: The Implications of Deep Cuts', *International Security*, vol. 13, no. 1, Summer 1988, pp. 90–133; Kenneth N. Waltz, 'Nuclear Myths and Political Realities', *American Political Science Review*, vol. 84, no. 3, September 1990, pp. 731–45; Charles L. Glaser, *Analyzing Strategic Nuclear Policy* (Princeton, NJ: Princeton University Press, 1990), ch. 6; Charles L. Glaser, 'The Instability of Small Numbers Revisited: Prospects for Disarmament and Nonproliferation', Conference on Rebuilding the NPT Consensus, Center for International Security and Cooperation, Stanford University, CA, 16–17 October 2007, http://iis-db.stanford.edu/pubs/22218/RebuildNPTConsensus.pdf. For histories of 'minimum deterrence' see Graham Barral, 'The Lost Tablets: An Analysis of the Concept of Minimum Deterrence', *Arms Control*, vol. 13, no. 1, April 1992, pp. 58–84; Jeffrey Lewis, 'Minimum Deterrence', *Bulletin of the Atomic Scientists*, vol. 64, no. 3, July–August 2008, pp. 38–41.

8 George Perkovich, 'Keeping up with the Nuclear Neighbours', *Nature*, vol. 458, no. 7,238, 2 April 2009, p. 574.

9 In addition to the nine states listed in Table 1, South Africa also built an arsenal of seven nuclear weapons (one of which was unfinished). It dismantled these weapons in the early 1990s.

10 The Obama administration's strengthened 'negative security assurance', which it has highlighted as the centrepiece of its efforts to reduce the role of nuclear weapons, is, in fact, only marginally stronger than similar pledges issued in 1978 and 1995.

11 George Perkovich *et al.*, *Universal Compliance: A Strategy for Nuclear Security*, 2007 edition (Washington DC: Carnegie Endowment for International Peace, 2007), http://carnegieendowment.org/files/univ_comp_rpt07_final1.pdf, pp. 137–38.

12 The Bush administration opposed the CTBT throughout its term. The Obama Administration supports the CTBT. However, it currently appears unlikely that this support will translate into legislative action.

13 See, for example, Jon Kyl and Richard Perle, 'Our Decaying Nuclear Deterrent', *Wall Street Journal*, 30 June 2009, http://online.wsj.com/article/SB124623202363966157.html.

14 Hillary R. Clinton, prepared statement to the hearings before the Committee on Foreign Relations of the United States Senate on 'The New START Treaty', S. HRG. 111-738, Washington, DC, 18 May 2010, http://foreign.senate.gov/download/?id=A0C2E5F0-8CB7-46B8-A3C1-014024059D16, p. 42.

15 Achilles Zaluar, 'A Realistic Approach to Nuclear Disarmament' in Perkovich and Acton (eds), *Abolishing Nuclear Weapons: A Debate*, p. 188.

16 The evidence so far is ambiguous. For example, the 2010 Non-proliferation Treaty Review Conference (regarded as an important test of the strategy) did produce a unanimous final document – but it contained very modest language, especially on non-proliferation. Advocates of the strategy could argue that non-nuclear-weapon states still have good reason to be skeptical of the American commitment to disarmament given that the Obama administration has not yet been able to fulfill key promises. New START, for instance, had not been ratified at the time of the Review Conference. More importantly, the prospect of CTBT

ratification – widely regarded as *the key indicator of progress* – is very slim. Critics of the administration's strategy could argue that non-nuclear weapon states are showing little interest in creative bargaining.

17   Donald H. Rumsfeld, prepared statement to the hearings before the Committee on Foreign Relations of the United States Senate on 'Treaty on Strategic Offensive Reduction: The Moscow Treaty', S. HRG. 107-622, Washington, DC, 17 July 2002, http://frwebgate.access.gpo.gov/cgi-bin/getdoc.cgi?dbname=107_senate_hearings&docid=f:81339.pdf, p. 85.

18   Robert G. Joseph, prepared statement to the hearings before the Committee on Foreign Relations of the United States Senate on 'The New START Treaty', S. HRG. 111-738, 24 June 2010, p. 361.

19   Joseph R. Biden Jr, 'The Case for Ratifying New Start', *Wall Street Journal*, 25 November 2010, http://online.wsj.com/article/SB10001424052748704074804575631051668226566.html.

20   Quoted in 'Senior Russian MP says New Start Better for Russia than U.S.', RIA Novosti, 7 January 2011, http://en.rian.ru/world/20110107/162068548.html.

21   See, for example, Sergei Karaganov, 'Nuclear Weapons in the Modern World', in *Nuclear Disarmament and Nonproliferation*, Report to the Trilateral Commission 64 (Washington DC, Paris and Tokyo: The Trilateral Commission, 2010), chapter 5.

22   Sergei M. Rogov, Viktor Esin, Pavel S. Zolotarev and Valeriy Yarynich, 'Sood'ba Stratyegichyeskih Vooroozhyeniy Poslye Pragi [The Fate of Strategic Arms after Prague]', *Nyezavisimoye Voyennoye Obozryeniye* [Independent Military Review], 27 August 2010, http://nvo.ng.ru/concepts/2010-08-27/1_strategic.html (in Russian); Vladimir Dvorkin, 'Reducing Russia's Reliance on Nuclear Weapons in Security Policies' in Cristina Hansell and William C. Potter (eds), *Engaging China and Russia on Nuclear Disarmament*, Occasional Paper 15 (Monterey, CA: James Martin Center for Nonproliferation Studies, Monterey Institute of International Studies, 2009), http://cns.miis.edu/opapers/op15/op15.pdf, pp. 89–102.

23   For their role in US doctrine see *Nuclear Posture Review Report*, pp. 15–17. For an analysis of their role in Russian doctrine see Nikolai Sokov, 'The New, 2010 Russian Military Doctrine: The Nuclear Angle', *CNS Feature Stories*, James Martin Center for Nonproliferation Studies, 5 February 2010, http://cns.miis.edu/stories/100205_russian_nuclear_doctrine.htm.

24   Thomas C. Schelling, *The Strategy of Conflict* (Cambridge, MA: Harvard University, 1960), p. 207. Italics in original.

25   Thomas C. Schelling, *Arms and Influence* (New Haven, CT: Yale University Press, 1966), pp. 248–51.

26   Freedman, 'Nuclear Disarmament', p. 146. See also Glenn A. Kent and David E. Thaler, *First-Strike Stability: A Methodology for Evaluating Strategic Forces*, R-3765-AF (Santa Monica, CA: RAND, 1989), p. 49.

27   *Nuclear Posture Review Report*, p. 29.

28   Colin Powell, prepared statement to the hearings before the Committee on Foreign Relations of the United States Senate on 'Treaty on Strategic Offensive Reduction', S. HRG. 107-622, 9 July 2002, p. 15.

29   Perkovich *et al.*, *Universal Compliance*, p. 138.

30 'Nuclear Posture Review [Excerpts]', 8 January 2002, http://www.globalsecurity.org/wmd/library/policy/dod/npr.htm.

31 Ibid.

32 See, for example, Thomas Scheber, 'Strategic Stability: Time for a Reality Check', International Journal, vol. 63, no. 4, Autumn 2008, pp. 903–04.

33 See, for example, Colin S. Gray, 'Strategic Stability Reconsidered', Daedalus, vol. 109, no. 4, Fall 1980, pp. 135–54; Keith B. Payne, The Fallacies of Cold War Deterrence and a New Direction (Lexington, KY: University Press of Kentucky, 2001), pp. 175–82; Keir A. Lieber and Daryl G. Press, 'The Nukes We Need: Preserving the American Deterrent', Foreign Affairs, vol. 88, no. 6, November–December 2009, pp. 39–51.

34 Stephen Prowse and Albert Wohlstetter, 'Stability in a World with More than Two Countries', in Sanford Lakoff (ed.), Beyond START?, IGCC Policy Paper 7 (University of California, Institute on Global Conflict and Cooperation, 1988), http://igcc.ucsd.edu/pdf/policypapers/pp07old.pdf, p. 46.

35 International Commission on Nuclear Non-proliferation and Disarmament, Eliminating Nuclear Threats: A Practical Agenda for Global Policymakers (Canberra/Tokyo: 2009), http://www.icnnd.org/reference/reports/ent/pdf/ICNND_Report-EliminatingNuclearThreats.pdf, p. 171.

36 'Fact Sheet: Increasing Transparency in the U.S. Nuclear Weapons Stockpile',
3 May 2010, http://www.defense.gov/npr/docs/10-05-03_Fact_Sheet_US_Nuclear_Transparency__FINAL_w_Date.pdf; Robert S. Norris and Hans M. Kristensen, 'Russian Nuclear Forces, 2010', Bulletin of the Atomic Scientists, vol. 66, no. 1, January–February 2010, p. 76.

37 The figure for the DPRK assumes it has produced between 52kg and 69kg of plutonium and has separated and fabricated it all into weapons, of which two have been used in tests. It is further assumed that the DPRK incurred high process losses of 20% and that each weapons contains 6kg of plutonium.

38 Robert S. Norris and Hans M. Kristensen, 'Global Nuclear Weapons Inventories, 1945–2010', Bulletin of the Atomic Scientists, vol. 66, no. 4, July–August 2010, pp. 81–2. Of course, the average yield of weapons in the stockpile is much larger now than it was then.

39 Remarks by US President Obama and President Medvedev of Russia at New START Treaty Signing Ceremony and Press Conference, Prague, 8 April 2010, http://www.whitehouse.gov/the-press-office/remarks-president-obama-and-president-medvedev-russia-new-start-treaty-signing-cere.

40 Robert S. Norris and Hans M. Kristensen, 'U.S. Nuclear Forces, 2010', Bulletin of the Atomic Scientists, vol. 66, no. 3, May–June 2010, p. 58; Norris and Kristensen, 'Russian Nuclear Forces, 2010', p. 74.

41 Nuclear Posture Review Report, p. 27.

Chapter One

1   Keir A. Lieber and Daryl G. Press, 'The End of MAD? The Nuclear Dimension of U.S. Primacy', *International Security*, vol. 30, no. 4, Spring 2006, pp. 7–44.

2   For example, McGeorge Bundy, 'To Cap the Volcano', *Foreign Affairs*, vol. 48, no. 1, October 1969, pp. 9–12; Kenneth N. Waltz, 'More May be Better', in Scott D. Sagan and Kenneth N. Waltz, *The Spread of Nuclear Weapons: A Debate Renewed* (New York: W. W. Norton & Company, 2003), chapter 1.

3   For example, Richard Rosecrance, *Strategic Deterrence Reconsidered*, Adelphi Paper 116 (London: The International Institute for Strategic Studies, 1975), pp. 2–3.

4   In 1969, Bundy claimed that in 'the real world of real political leaders – whether here or in the Soviet Union – a decision that would bring even one hydrogen bomb on one city of one's own country would be recognized in advance as a catastrophic blunder; ten bombs on ten cities would be a disaster beyond history.' Bundy, 'To Cap the Volcano', p. 10.

5   Herman Kahn was the leading theorist from the damage-limitation school of deterrence. In 1960, he suggested that the United States 'should be able to distinguish (and choose, perhaps) between a country which survives a war with, say, 150 million people and a gross national product (GNP) of $300 billion a year, and a nation which emerges with only 50 million people and a GNP of $10 billion.' Herman Kahn, *On Thermonuclear War* (Princeton, NJ: Princeton University Press, 1960), p. 19.

6   Ernest R. May, John D. Steinbruner and Thomas W. Wolfe, *History of the Strategic Arms Competition 1945–1972, Part I* (Office of the Secretary of Defense Historical Office, 1981), http://www.dod.gov/pubs/foi/reading_room/226.pdf, p. 341.

7   Quoted in Lewis, 'Minimum Deterrence', p. 38.

8   T. V. Paul, 'Nuclear Taboo and War Initiation in Regional Conflicts', *Journal of Conflict Resolution*, vol. 39, no. 4, December 1995, pp. 708–11.

9   Avery Goldstein, *Deterrence and Security in the 21st Century: China, Britain, France and the Enduring Legacy of the Nuclear Revolution* (Stanford, CA: Stanford University Press, 2000), chapter 4.

10 Jeffrey Lewis, *The Minimum Means of Reprisal: China's Search for Security in the Nuclear Age* (Cambridge, MA: MIT Press, 2007), pp. 3–18.

11 Lyle J. Goldstein, *Preventive Attack and Weapons of Mass Destruction: A Comparative Historical Analysis* (Stanford, CA: Stanford University Press, 2006), pp. 15–18 and 84–8.

12 Sagan, 'More Will be Worse', in Sagan and Waltz, *The Spread of Nuclear Weapons*, pp. 55–59.

13 Frank Miller, 'Disarmament and Deterrence: A Practitioner's View' in Perkovich and Acton (eds), *Abolishing Nuclear Weapons: A Debate*, pp. 153–54.

14 Payne, 'How Much is Enough?', p. 6. For the argument that nuclear 'bunker busting' adds little to deterrence see Charles L. Glaser and Steve Fetter, 'Counterforce Revisited: Assessing the Nuclear Posture Review's New Missions', *International Security*, vol. 30, no. 2, Fall 2005, pp. 90–95.

15 Hans M. Kristensen, 'Obama and the Nuclear War Plan', Federation of the American Scientists Issue Brief,

February 2010, http://www.fas.org/programs/ssp/nukes/publications1/WarPlanIssueBrief2010.pdf,p. 6.

[16] Interview with former senior US official, Washington, DC, October 2009.

[17] See, for example, Richard Pipes, 'Why the Soviet Union Thinks it Could Fight and Win a Nuclear War', *Commentary*, vol. 64, no. 1, July 1977, pp. 21–34.

[18] Intelligence Community Experiment in Competitive Analysis, *Soviet Strategic Objectives: An Alternative View: Report of Team B* (Washington, DC: CIA, December 1976), pp. 25–26.

[19] John G. Hines, Ellis M. Mishulovich and John F. Shull, *Soviet Intentions 1965–1985*, Volume I, *An Analytical Comparison of U.S.–Soviet Assessments During the Cold War* (McLean, VA: BDM Federal, 1995), available from http://www.gwu.edu/~nsarchiv/nukevault/ebb285/, pp. 24–25.

[20] *Ibid.*, p. 27.

[21] Norris and Kristensen, 'Global Nuclear Weapons Inventories, 1945–2010', p. 81.

[22] See, for example, Pipes, 'Why the Soviet Union Thinks it Could Fight and Win a Nuclear War', p. 34.

[23] David Holloway, *Stalin and the Bomb: The Soviet Union and Atomic Energy, 1939–1956* (New Haven, CT: Yale University Press, 1994), p. 238. For Soviet estimates of the size of the US stockpile see p. 240.

[24] *Ibid.*

[25] *Ibid.*, p. 271.

[26] Cold War historian John Lewis Gaddis has argued that if the US had possessed a sufficiently large arsenal to be able to destroy the Soviet Union without threat of retaliation in the long term, Stalin would not have been able to engage in aggressive behaviour. This may be right but this strategy ceased to be even theoretically viable after the Soviet Union developed a survivable second-strike capability. John Lewis Gaddis, *We Now Know: Rethinking Cold War History* (Oxford: Clarendon Press, 1997), pp. 96–99.

[27] Victor Gobarev, 'Soviet Military Plans and Actions During the First Berlin Crisis, 1948–49', *Journal of Slavic Military Studies*, vol. 10, no. 3, September 1997, p. 5.

[28] See, for example, Richard K. Betts, *Nuclear Blackmail and Nuclear Balance* (Washington, DC: Brookings Institution, 1987), pp. 23–31. Note that the controversial question of whether the deployment of American 'nuclear-capable' B-29 bombers to the UK was interpreted by Stalin as a signal is distinct from the question of whether Stalin was deterred by US nuclear weapons at all.

[29] As numbers come down the ABM system around Moscow might become an increasing concern to the United States. To combat this system, the US could focus on the development of countermeasures, exactly as the UK did in the 1970s and 1980s.

[30] I. C. Oelrich, 'Sizing Post-Cold War Nuclear Forces', Institute for Defense Analyses, P-3650, October 2001, http://www.fas.org/programs/ssp/nukes/doctrine/szngnuclearforces.pdf, pp. 15–16.

[31] Michael Quinlan, *Thinking About Nuclear Weapons: Principles, Problems, Prospects* (Oxford: Oxford University Press, 2009), pp. 124–26.

[32] *Ibid.*, p. 125.

[33] Janne E. Nolan, *An Elusive Consensus: Nuclear Weapons and American Security After the Cold War* (Washington DC: Brookings Institution Press, 1999),

pp. 48–49. The author has heard this comment in many conversations with US officials more recently.

34 May, Bing and Steinbruner, 'Strategic Arsenals after START', pp. 125–31.

35 Lynn Eden, 'The US Nuclear Arsenal and Zero: Sizing and Planning for Use–Past, Present and Future', in Catherine Kelleher and Judith Reppy (eds), *Getting to Zero: The Path to Nuclear Disarmament* (Stanford, CA: Stanford University Press, forthcoming).

36 For related discussions see Michael J. Mazarr, 'Military Targets for a Minimum Deterrent: After the Cold War How Much is Enough?', *Journal of Strategic Studies*, vol. 15, no. 2, June 1992, pp. 147–71; Hans M. Kristensen, Robert S. Norris and Ivan Oelrich, *From Counterforce to Minimal Deterrence: A New Nuclear Policy on the Path Toward Eliminating Nuclear Weapons*, Occasional Paper 7 (Washington DC: Federation of American Scientists/Natural Resources Defense Council, 2009), http://www.fas.org/pubs/_docs/OccasionalPaper7.pdf, p. 31–41.

37 Alexei Arbatov and Sergey Oznobishchev, 'Pushki–Pod Kontrolem, Kompromiss Dostignut [Guns: Under Control, Compromise Reached], *Nyezavisimoye Voyennoye Obozryeniye*, 9 July 2010, http://nvo.

ng.ru/concepts/2010-07-09/1_pushki.html (in Russian).

38 Dmitri Trenin, 'Russian Perspectives on the Global Elimination of Nuclear Weapons', in Barry Blechman (ed.), *Unblocking the Road to Zero: Russia and the United States* (Washington DC: The Henry L. Stimson Center, 2009), http://www.stimson.org/images/uploads/research-pdfs/Russia_US_Format_FINAL.pdf, pp. 5–7.

39 Rogov, Esin, Zolotarev and Yarynich, 'Sood'ba Stratyegichyeskih Vooroozhyeniy Poslye Pragi'.

40 Sergey Lavrov, remarks to the State Duma, Moscow, 14 January 2011, http://www.mid.ru/brp_4.nsf/0/B4B970B7D9B7FAD9C3257818005CDBD2 (in Russian).

41 Samuel Glasstone and Philip J. Dolan, *The Effects of Nuclear Weapons*, Third Edition (Washington, DC: US Department of Defense and US Energy Research and Development Administration, 1977), para. 9.13; 'Chernobyl Accident', World Nuclear Association, November 2009, http://www.world-nuclear.org/info/chernobyl/info7.html.

42 This point was made in three separate interviews with Russian analysts and former military officers, Moscow, November 2009. See also Schelling, *Arms and Influence*, pp. 109–16.

Chapter Two

1   'Japan, U.S. to Launch Talks on "Nuclear Umbrella"', *Global Security Newswire*, 20 July 2009, http://gsn.nti.org/gsn/nw_20090720_2855.php; 'Joint Vision for the Alliance of the United States of America and the Republic of Korea', Washington DC, 16 June 2009, http://www.whitehouse.gov/the_press_office/Joint-vision-for-the-alliance-of-the-United-States-of-America-and-the-Republic-of-Korea/.

2   For example, National Institute for Public Policy, *U.S. Extended Deterrence and Assurance for Allies in Northeast Asia* (National Institute Press, 2010), http://www.nipp.org/National Institute Press/Current Publications/PDF/US%20 Extend-Deter-for print.pdf, especially pp. 35–7.

3   'Active Engagement, Modern Defense: Strategic Concept for the Defense and Security of the Members of the North Atlantic Treaty Organisation', [2010], http://www.nato.int/lisbon2010/strategic-concept-2010-eng.pdf, para. 26.

4   Franklin Miller, George Robertson and Kori Schake, 'Germany Opens Pandora's Box', Briefing Note, Centre for European Reform, February 2010, http://www.cer.org.uk/pdf/bn_pandora_final_8feb10.pdf. Of course, securing a reciprocal arrangement on tactical nuclear weapons would require NATO to recognise and accommodate Russian concerns.

5   For a discussion about how the US should engage with its allies see James M. Acton, *Low Numbers: A Practical Path to Deep Nuclear Reductions* (Washington DC: Carnegie Endowment for International Peace, forthcoming), chapter 2.

6   For example, Paul H. Nitze, 'Assuring Strategic Stability in an Era of Détente', *Foreign Affairs*, vol. 54, no. 2, January 1976, pp. 212–14. For a contrary view see Robert Jervis, 'Why Nuclear Superiority Doesn't Matter', *Political Science Quarterly*, vol. 94, no. 4, Winter 1979–80, pp. 623–25.

7   Katsuhisa Furukawa, 'Nuclear Option, Arms Control, and Extended Deterrence: In Search of a New Framework for Japan's Nuclear Policy' in Benjamin L. Self and Jeffrey W. Thompson (eds), *Japan's Nuclear Option: Security, Politics, and Policy in the 21st Century* (Washington DC: Henry L. Stimson Center, 2003), p. 118.

8   The classic discussion is Kahn, *On Thermonuclear War*, pp. 27–36.

9   Whether damage limitation ceased to be a guide for operational planning is a somewhat controversial question. See, for example, Earl C. Ravenal, 'Counterforce and Alliance: The Ultimate Connection', *International Security*, vol. 6, no. 4, Spring 1982, pp. 26–43.

10 Shinichi Ogawa, 'Missile Defense and Deterrence', *NIDS Security Reports*, no. 3, March 2002, available from http://www.nids.go.jp/english/publication/kiyo/e2001.html, p. 34.

11 National Institute for Defense Studies, *East Asian Strategic Review 2010* (Tokyo: The Japan Times, 2010), available from http://www.nids.go.jp/english/publication/east-asian/e2010.html, p. 33.

12 William J. Perry *et al.*, *America's Strategic Posture: The Final Report of the Congressional Commission on the Strategic Posture of the United States* (Washington DC: United States Institute of Peace

Press, 2009), http://www.usip.org/files/
America's_Strategic_Posture_Auth_
Ed.pdf, p. 23. See also Baker Spring,
'Congressional Commission Should
Recommend "Damage Limitation"
Strategy', Heritage Foundation, 14
August 2008, http://www.heritage.
org/Research/Reports/2008/08/
Congressional-Commission-Should-
Recommend-Damage-Limitation-
Strategy#_ftnref17; Payne, 'How Much
is Enough?', pp. 13–14.

13 Lieber and Press, 'The Nukes We
Need'; Payne, *The Fallacies of Cold War
Deterrence and a New Direction*, pp.
175–82.

14 Peter C. W. Flory, 'Just the Facts',
Foreign Affairs, vol. 85, no. 5,
September–October 2006, pp.
149–50; Keith B. Payne, 'A Matter of
Record', *Foreign Affairs*, vol. 85, no. 5,
September–October 2006, pp. 150–52.
See also Austin Long, *Deterrence from
Cold War to Long War: Lessons from
Six Decades of RAND Research* (Santa
Monica, CA: RAND Corporation,
2008), http://www.rand.org/pubs/
monographs/2008/RAND_MG636.pdf,
pp. 25–43.

15 US Department of Defense, *Deterrence
Operations: Joint Operating Concept*,
version 2.0 (December 2006), http://
www.dtic.mil/futurejointwarfare/
concepts/do_joc_v20.doc, p. 27.

16 Kristensen, 'Obama and the Nuclear
War Plan', pp. 7–10.

17 *Nuclear Posture Review Report*, p. 34.

18 Lieber and Press, 'The Nukes we
Need'.

19 This figure represents 5–10 DF-3
(CSS-2) TELs, 75–85 DF-21 (CSS-5)
TELs, 10–15 DF-31A TELs and fewer
than 10 DF-31 TELs. The DF-4 (CSS-3)
has not been included since these
missiles are not truly mobile (they are

probably stored in caves and rolled
out to launch). Office of the Secretary
of Defense, *Military and Security
Developments Involving the People's
Republic of China 2010* (Department of
Defense, 2010), http://www.defense.
gov/pubs/pdfs/2010_CMPR_Final.pdf,
p. 66.

20 Norris and Kristensen, 'Russian
Nuclear Forces, 2010', p. 76.

21 For discussions of the challenges of
destroying mobile missiles see Dennis
M. Gormley, 'The Path to Deep Nuclear
Reductions: Dealing with American
Conventional Superiority', *Proliferation
Papers* 29, Fall 2009, http://www.ifri.
org/downloads/pp29gormley1.pdf,
pp. 21–23; James M. Acton, 'Managing
Vulnerability', *Foreign Affairs*, vol. 89,
no. 2, March–April 2010, pp. 146–48;
Jan Lodal, 'The Counterforce Fantasy',
Foreign Affairs, vol. 89, no. 2, March–
April 2010, pp. 145–46; Gerson, 'No
First Use', pp. 25–30.

22 Barry D. Watts and Thomas A. Keaney,
'Effects and Effectiveness' in *Gulf War
Air Power Survey*, Volume II, Part II
(Washington DC: 1993), http://www.
airforcehistory.hq.af.mil/Publications/
fulltext/gulf_war_air_power_survey-
vol2.pdf, pp. 330–32.

23 Gormley, 'The Path to Deep Nuclear
Reductions', p. 23. (I do not mean to
imply that Gormley is an advocate of
damage limitation, just that I discov-
ered this example through his work.)

24 Noam Ophir, 'Look Not to the Skies:
The IAF vs. Surface-to-Surface Rocket
Launchers', *Strategic Assessment*,
November 2006, vol. 9, no. 3, http://
www.inss.org.il/publications.
php?cat=21&incat=&read=86#_ftnref7,
p. 6.

25 Keir A. Lieber and Daryl G. Press,
'Lieber and Press Reply', *Foreign Affairs*,

vol. 89, no. 2, March–April 2010, p. 152.

26   This assumes that a mobile missile can move at about 15 miles per hour. Glaser and Fetter, 'Counterforce Revisited', p. 97.

27   International Institute for Strategic Studies, *The Military Balance 2010* (Abingdon: Routledge for the IISS, 2010), p. 401.

28   *The People's Liberation Army Navy: A Modern Navy with Chinese Characteristics* (Suitland, MD: Office of Naval Intelligence, 2009), http://www.fas.org/irp/agency/oni/pla-navy.pdf, p. 23.

29   *The People's Liberation Army Navy*, p. 22.

30   With four SSBNs China might be able to put two at sea in a crisis.

31   See, for example, Payne, *The Fallacies of Cold War Deterrence and a New Direction*, pp. 175–82.

32   Philip E. Coyle, 'The Future of Missile Defense Testing', prepared testimony to the Subcommittee on Strategic Forces, Committee on Armed Services of the US House of Representatives, Washington, DC, 25 February 2009, http://www.cdi.org/pdfs/CoyleHASCfull2_25_091.pdf.

33   *Military and Security Developments Involving the People's Republic of China 2010*, p. 34.

34   *Ibid*, p. 66.

35   Hans M. Kristensen, Robert S. Norris and Matthew G. McKinzie, *Chinese Nuclear Forces and U.S. War Planning*, (Washington DC: Federation of American Scientists/Natural Resources Defense Council, 2006), http://www.fas.org/nuke/guide/china/Book2006.pdf, pp. 104–06.

36   Betts, *Nuclear Blackmail and Nuclear Balance*, p. 96.

37   Marc Trachtenberg, *History and Strategy* (Princeton, NJ: Princeton University Press, 1991), chapter 5.

38   Hope M. Harrison, *Ulbricht and the Concrete 'Rose': New Archival Evidence on the Dynamics of Soviet–East German Relations and the Berlin Crisis, 1958–61*, Working Paper 5, Cold War International History Project (Washington DC: Woodrow Wilson Center for Scholars, 1993), http://wilsoncenter.org/topics/pubs/ACFB81.pdf, p. 53.

39   Honoré M. Catudal, *Kennedy and the Berlin Wall Crisis: A Case Study in US Decision Making* (Berlin: Springer-Verlag, 1980), p. 211.

40   Fred Kaplan, 'JKF's First Strike Plan', *Atlantic Monthly*, vol. 288, no. 3, October 2001, pp. 81–6.

41   Carl Kaysen to General Maxwell Taylor, military representative to the president, 'Strategic Air Planning and Berlin', 5 September 1961, Top Secret, excised copy, with cover memoranda to General Lemnitzer, http://www.gwu.edu/~nsarchiv/NSAEBB/NSAEBB56/BerlinC1.pdf.

42   Betts, *Nuclear Blackmail and Nuclear Balance*, p. 102.

43   Memorandum from Maxwell D. Taylor to General Lemnitzer, 19 September 1961, enclosing memorandum on 'Strategic Air Planning', Top Secret, http://www.gwu.edu/~nsarchiv/NSAEBB/NSAEBB56/BerlinC3.pdf.

44   Minutes from the Discussion Between the Delegation of the PRL [People's Republic of Poland] and the Government of the USSR, 25 October–10 November 1958, reproduced in Douglas Selvage, 'Khrushchev's November 1958 Berlin Ultimatum: New Evidence from the Polish Archives', *Cold War International History Project Bulletin*, no. 11, Winter 1998, http://www.wilsoncenter.org/index.cfm?topic_id=1409&fuseaction=topics.

publications&group_id=13422, p. 202.

45 Betts, *Nuclear Blackmail and Nuclear Balance*, p. 107; Aleksandr Fursenko and Timothy Naftali, *Khrushchev's Cold War: The Inside Story of an American Adversary* (New York: W.W. Norton and Company, 2006), pp. 356–57.

46 Vladislav M. Zubok, *Khrushchev and the Berlin Crisis (1958–1962)*, Working Paper 6, Cold War International History Project (Washington DC: Woodrow Wilson Center for Scholars, 1993), http://www.wilsoncenter.org/

topics/pubs/ACFB7D.pdf, p. 26.

47 Quoted in James L. Schoff, *Realigning Priorities: The U.S.–Japan Alliance and the Future of Extended Deterrence* (Cambridge, MA: Institute for Foreign Policy Analysis, 2009), http://www.ifpa.org/pdf/RealignPriorities.pdf.

48 Michael S. Gerson, 'Conventional Deterrence in the Second Nuclear Age', *Parameters*, vol. 39, 2009, pp. 38–39.

49 Keith B. Payne, 'Post Cold-War Deterrence and a Taiwan Crisis', *China Brief*, vol. 1, no. 5, 2001.

Chapter Three

1 Alexei Arbatov, Vladimir Dvorkin, Alexander Pikaev and Sergey Oznobishchev, *Strategic Stability After the Cold War* (Moscow: IMEMO, 2010), http://www.posse.gatech.edu/sites/default/files/IMEMO_Strategic Stability after the Cold War.pdf, p. 27.

2 Gerson, 'No First Use', pp. 35–39.

3 For excellent overviews see Rogov, Esin, Zolotarev and Yarynich, 'Sood'ba Stratyegichyeskih Vooroozhyeniy Poslye Pragi'; Arbatov, Dvorkin, Pikaev and Oznobishchev, *Strategic Stability After the Cold War*, pp. 18–25; Anatoli S. Diakov, Timur T. Kadyshev and Eugene V. Miasnikov, 'Further Reductions of Nuclear Weapons', Center for Arms Control, Energy & Environmental Studies, Moscow Institute of Physics and Technology, 3 February 2010, http://www.armscontrol.ru/pubs/en/post-start-reductions-en.pdf.

4 Yevgeny Miasnikov, 'The Counterforce Potential of Precision-Guided Munitions' in Alexei Arbatov and Vladimir Dvorkin (eds), *Nuclear*

Proliferation: New Technologies, Weapons, Treaties (Moscow: Carnegie Moscow Center, 2009), http://www.carnegieendowment.org/files/12574Blok_YadernoyeRaspr_Eng_fin1.pdf, chapter 5; Dvorkin, 'Reducing Russia's Reliance on Nuclear Weapons in Security Policies', p. 100.

5 Interview with former Russian official, Italy, January 2010.

6 On anti-submarine warfare see Arbatov, Dvorkin, Pikaev and Oznobishchev, *Strategic Stability After the Cold War*, pp. 23–24.

7 Gormley, 'The Path to Deep Nuclear Reductions', pp. 21–23 and pp. 35–37.

8 Richard Weitz, 'Illusive Visions and Practical Realities: Russia, NATO and Missile Defence', *Survival*, vol. 52, no. 4, August–September 2010, pp. 103–12.

9 Transcript of Remarks and Response to Media Questions by Russian Foreign Minister Sergey Lavrov at Press Conference in Relation to the Upcoming Signing of a Treaty between Russia and the USA on Measures to

Further Reduction and Limitation of Strategic Offensive Arms, Moscow, 6 April 2010.

10   *Ibid.*; Sergei Kislyak, remarks on 'International Perspectives on the Nuclear Posture Review', Carnegie Endowment for International Peace, Washington, DC, http://www.carnegieendowment.org/events/?fa=eventDetail&id=2842, 21 April 2010.

11   *Nuclear Posture Review Report*, pp. 19–30.

12   Nitze, 'Assuring Strategic Stability in an Era of Détente'.

13   George H. Quester, 'Through the Nuclear Strategic Looking Glass, or Reflections off the Window of Vulnerability', *Journal of Conflict Resolution*, vol. 31, no. 4, December 1987, pp. 725–37; Pavel Podvig, 'The Window of Vulnerability that Wasn't: Soviet Military Buildup in the 1970s – A Research Note', *International Security*, vol. 33, no. 1, Summer 2008, pp. 118–38.

14   Peter Vincent Pry, *War Scare: Russia and America on the Nuclear Brink* (Westport, CT: Praeger, 1999), pp. 41–42.

15   Robert M. Gates, *From the Shadows* (New York: Simon & Schuster, 1996), p. 270.

16   *Ibid*, p. 273.

17   Fursenko and Naftali, *Khrushchev's Cold War*, p. 424.

18   For the case that US strategic superiority did help lead to Khrushchev's climb down see Trachtenberg, *History and Strategy*, pp. 253–58.

19   These are considered further in Acton, *Low Numbers*, chapter 1. For detailed analyses of the next round of US–Russia arms control see the forthcoming report of the Next Generation Working Group on US-Russia Arms Control; Steven Pifer, *The Next Round:* *The United States and Nuclear Arms Reductions After New START*, Arms Control Series Paper 4 (Brookings, 2010), http://www.brookings.edu/~/media/Files/rc/articles/2010/12_arms_control_pifer/12_arms_control_pifer.pdf; Rogov, Esin, Zolotarev and Yarynich, 'Sood'ba Stratyegichyeskih Vooroozhyeniy Poslye Pragi'.

20   Kislyak, remarks on 'International Perspectives on the Nuclear Posture Review'.

21   Lakoff (ed.), *Beyond START?*, pp. 16–19.

22   Keith B. Payne, 'Evaluating the U.S.-Russia Nuclear Deal', *Wall Street Journal*, 8 April 2010, http://online.wsj.com/article/SB10001424052702303720604575169532920779888.html.

23   For instance, US Defense Secretary Robert Gates has said that 'if we go down significantly in the number of nuclear weapons that we have deployed, the question is whether the traditional triad makes sense anymore and I think we have to address that.' Remarks by Robert Gates, Maxwell Air Force Base, AL, 15 April 2009, http://www.defense.gov/transcripts/transcript.aspx?transcriptid=4403.

24   Dana J. Johnson, Christopher J. Bowie and Robert P. Haffa, *Triad, Dyad, Monad? Shaping the US Nuclear Force for the Future*, Mitchell Paper 5 (Mitchell Institute Press, 2009), http://www.afa.org/mitchell/reports/MP5_Triad_1209.pdf.

25   Of course, a monad could consist purely of bombers. Steve Andreasen, 'Reagan was Right: Let's Ban Ballistic Missiles', *Survival*, vol. 46, no. 1, Spring 2004, pp. 117–29. Although theoretically interesting, such an option seems extremely unlikely to be realised in practice.

26 For a related discussion in the US–China context see Jeffrey G. Lewis, 'Chinese Nuclear Posture and Force Modernization', *Nonproliferation Review*, vol. 16, no. 2, July 2009, pp. 205–06.

27 This tendency might be further exacerbated because the verification measures that would probably be needed to enable deep cuts might give the US information that would make a first strike easier.

28 Interview with former senior Russian military officer, Moscow, November 2009.

29 See, for example, 'Baucus, Tester Team up with Colleagues to Push Support for ICBMs', 29 September 2009, http://tester.senate.gov/Newsroom/pr_092909_icbms.cfm.

Chapter Four

1 Warheads have never been subject to verifiable destruction and developing provisions for doing so is an important new challenge for US–Russian arms control. For a recent review of the subject see David Cliff, Hassan Elbahtimy and Andreas Persbo, *Verifying Warhead Dismantlement: Past, Present, Future*, Verification Matters 9 (London: Verification Research, Training and Information Centre (VERTIC), 2010), http://www.vertic.org/media/assets/Publications/VM9.pdf.

2 A notable exception is Glaser, *Analyzing Strategic Nuclear Policy*, pp. 173–77. For a partial reassessment see Glaser, 'The Instability of Small Numbers Revisited'.

3 Scott D. Sagan, *Moving Targets: Nuclear Strategy and National Security* (Princeton, NJ: Princeton University Press, 1989), chapter 1. The distinction between war-fighting and 'coercion' is made in Schelling, *Arms and Influence*, pp. 1–6.

4 R.D. Little, *The History of Air Force Participation in the Atomic Energy Program, 1943–1953*, Volume II, *Foundations of an Atomic Air Force and Operation Sandstone, 1946–1948* (Air University Historical Liaison Office, [1955]), p. 248.

5 David Alan Rosenberg, 'The Origins of Overkill: Nuclear Weapons and American Strategy, 1945–1960', *International Security*, vol. 7, no. 4, Spring 1983, pp. 15–18.

6 By the 1970s about 1,600 strategic warheads (and many more tactical ones) were probably assigned to what, by then, was known as 'other military targets'. Sagan, *Moving Targets*, Table 1.3.

7 This is not the same arms race mechanism that is famously critiqued in Albert Wohlstetter, 'Racing Forward? Or Ambling Back?', in Robert Conquest et al., *Defending America* (New York: Basic Books, 1977), pp. 110–68.

8 Rosenberg, 'The Origins of Overkill', p. 66 and p. 50. He adds that the growth in targets was exacerbated by 'poor intelligence' leading to 'creative guesswork'.

9 Eden, 'The US Nuclear Arsenal and Zero'.

10 Ted Greenwood, *Making the MIRV: A Study of Defense Decision Making*

(Cambridge, MA: Ballinger Publishing Company, 1975), especially pp. 49–50.

11   Desmond Ball, *Politics and Force Levels: The Strategic Missile Program of the Kennedy Administration* (Berkeley, CA: University of California Press, 1980). For the military's 1961 'wish list' see pp. 192–93.

12   Hines, Mishulovich, and Shull, *Soviet Intentions 1965–1985*, p. 61.

13   Interview with former senior Russian military officer, Moscow, November 2009; Interview with former Russian official, Italy, January 2010. For a rare public indication of Russian concerns about China see Stephen J. Blank, *Russia and Arms Control: Are There Opportunities for the Obama Administration?* (Carlisle, PA: Strategic Studies Institute, U.S. Army War College, 2009), https://www.strategicstudiesinstitute.army.mil/pdffiles/PUB908.pdf, pp. 53–57.

14   James N. Miller, 'Zero and Minimal Nuclear Weapons', in Joseph S. Nye, Graham T. Allison and Albert Carnesale (eds), *Fateful Visions: Avoiding Nuclear Catastrophe* (Cambridge, MA: Ballinger Publishing Company, 1988), pp. 20–21.

15   For example, Robert A. Pape, *Bombing to Win: Air Power and Coercion in War* (Ithaca, NY: Cornell University Press, 1996), chapter 5.

16   For example, Rosemary J. Foot, 'Nuclear Coercion and the Ending of the Korean Conflict', *International Security*, vol. 13, no. 3, Winter 1988–1989, pp. 92–112; Appu K. Soman, *Double-Edged Sword: Nuclear Diplomacy in Unequal Conflicts: The United States and China, 1950–1958* (Westport, CT:

Praeger, 2000), chapter 3; Chen Jian, *Mao's China and the Cold War* (Chapel Hill, NC: University of North Carolina Press, 2001), chapter 4. I am grateful to Elbridge Colby for drawing my attention to this literature.

17   Scott D. Sagan and Jeremi Suri, 'The Madman Nuclear Alert: Secrecy, Signaling, and Safety in October 1969', *International Security*, vol. 27, no. 4, Spring 2003, pp. 150–83. More generally, see Betts, *Nuclear Blackmail and Nuclear Balance*.

18   Pape, *Bombing to Win*, p. 173.

19   In connection with abolition this point is made in Thomas C. Schelling, 'The Role of Deterrence in Total Disarmament', *Foreign Affairs*, vol. 40, no. 3, April 1962, pp. 392–406.

20   John D. Immele and Richard L. Wagner, 'The US Nuclear Weapon Infrastructure and a Stable Global Nuclear Weapons Regime', draft, LA-UR-09-00339, 19 January 2009, http://www.lanl.gov/conferences/sw/2009/docs/Immele_Wagner_2009.pdf.

21   Stephen M. Meyer, 'Verification and the ICBM Shell-Game', *International Security*, vol. 4, no. 2, Autumn 1979, p. 48.

22   Aleksandr Fursenko and Timothy Naftali, *"One Hell of a Gamble": Khrushchev, Castro, and Kennedy 1958–1964* (New York: W.W. Norton & Company, 1997), p. 171.

23   Providing extended deterrence to Cuba also played a role.

24   Richard Ned Lebow and Janice Gross Stein, *We All Lost the Cold War* (Princeton, NJ: Princeton University Press, 1994), p. 59.

Chapter Five

1   Important exceptions include Richard Rosecrance (ed)., *The Future of the International Strategic System* (San Francisco, CA: Chandler Publishing Company, 1972); Rosecrance, *Strategic Deterrence Reconsidered*, pp. 27–33.

2   Hoeber, 'How Little is Enough?', p. 64; Henry Sokolski, 'Avoiding a Nuclear Crowd', *Policy Review*, no. 155, June and July 2009, http://www.hoover.org/publications/policy-review/article/5534.

3   Arms race stability might be somewhat lower. For instance, an equilibrium between two states might be disturbed if one of them entered into an arms race with a third. Whether this is occurring today with Pakistan, India and China is debatable.

4   Rosecrance, *Strategic Deterrence Reconsidered*, pp. 28–29. For a discussion of the special case of pivotal deterrence (largely based on non-nuclear examples) see Timothy W. Crawford, *Pivotal Deterrence: Third-Party Statecraft and the Pursuit of Peace* (Ithaca, NY: Cornell University Press, 2003).

5   Miller, 'Zero and Minimal Nuclear Weapons', p. 19.

6   William Burr and Jeffrey T. Richelson, 'Whether to "Strangle the Baby in the Cradle": The United States and the Chinese Nuclear Program, 1960–64', *International Security*, vol. 25, no. 3, Winter 2000–2001, pp. 67–72 and pp. 86–88.

7   Henry Kissinger, *White House Years* (Boston, MA: Little, Brown and Company, 1979), p. 182.

8   Two separate interviews with former senior Russian military officers, Moscow, November 2009; Interview with former Russian official, Italy, January 2010.

9   Sergey Lavrov, 'New START Treaty in the Global Security Matrix: The Political Dimension', *Mezhdunarodnaya Zhizn*, no. 7, July 2010. Official translation available from Information and Press Department of the Ministry of Foreign Affairs of the Russian Federation, http://www.mid.ru/brp_4.nsf/e78a48070f128a7b43256999005bcbb3/25909cfe1bbd1c6ec325777500339245?OpenDocument, 2 August 2010.

10 Three separate interviews with senior Indian military officers (two retired, one serving), New Delhi, April 2010.

11 For a rare example from the academic literature see Brad Roberts, 'Nuclear Multipolarity and Stability', Institute for Defense Analyses, D-2539, November 2000, http://www.globalsecurity.org/wmd/library/report/2000/d2539dtra.doc, p. 30.

12 Two separate interviews with senior Indian military officers (one retired, one serving), New Delhi, April 2010.

13 Interview with former senior Japanese official, Washington, DC, April 2010.

14 Roberts, 'On Order, Stability, and Nuclear Abolition', p. 167. See also the comments by Rumsfeld during the hearing before the Committee on Foreign Relations of the United States Senate on 'Treaty on Strategic Offensive Reduction: The Moscow Treaty', S. HRG. 107-622, 17 July 2002, p. 111.

15 Kyl and Perle, 'Our Decaying Nuclear Deterrent'.

16 Perkovich and Acton, *Abolishing Nuclear Weapons*, pp. 39–40.

17 *Nuclear Posture Review Report*, p. 41.

18 For example, Gordon G. Chang, 'START-ing Without China', *Wall*

Street Journal, 27 January 2010, http://
online.wsj.com/article/SB1000142405
2748703906204575027821767691054.
html.

19 One possible vision for a multilateral
process is sketched out in Acton, *Low
Numbers*, chapter 4.

20 Author conversations with Chinese
officials, 2009–10.

Conclusions

1 The arms-control path to low numbers
is considered in detail in Acton, *Low
Numbers*.

2 For a more detailed discussion of the
next round of arms control, see the
references in Chapter Three, endnote
19.

3 For an excellent discussion of the
background to these events and the
options for moving forward see Anne
Witkowsky, Sherman Garnett and Jeff
McCausland, *Salvaging the Conventional
Armed Forces in Europe Treaty Regime:
Options for Washington*, Arms Control
Series Paper 2 (Brookings, 2010), http://
www.brookings.edu/~/media/Files/
rc/papers/2010/03_armed_forces_
europe_treaty/03_armed_forces_
europe_treaty.pdf.

4 These efforts have not been talked
about much in public. See Micah
Zenko, *Toward Deeper Reductions in U.S.
and Russian Nuclear Weapons*, Council
Special Report 57 (New York: Council
on Foreign Relations, 2010), http://
www.cfr.org/content/publications/
attachments/US-Russia_Nuclear_
CSR57.pdf, p. 10

5 Trenin, 'Russian Perspectives on
the Global Elimination of Nuclear
Weapons', p. 14.

6 Kwon Hyuk-chul, 'S. Korea-U.S.
to Organize a Joint Committee for
Extending Nuclear Deterrence', *The

Hankyoreh, 9 October 2010, http://
english.hani.co.kr/arti/english_
edition/e_northkorea/443035.html;
'Japan, US to Hold Talks on "Nuclear
Umbrella"', AFP, 7 July 2009, http://
www.google.com/hostednews/
afp/article/ALeqM5gDf27IKitrr_
RZoJ5wbv1ZaUOJYw.

7 See, for example, Josh Rogin, 'Heritage
Targets Republican Senators who
Might Favor New START', *The Cable*,
4 November 2010, http://thecable.
foreignpolicy.com/posts/2010/11/04/
heritage_targets_republican_
senators_who_might_favor_new_
start; Mitt Romney, 'Obama's Worst
Foreign-Policy Mistake', *Washington
Post*, 6 July 2010, http://www.
washingtonpost.com/wp-dyn/content/
article/2010/07/05/AR2010070502657.
html.

8 'CNN Poll: Three-Quarters say Ratify
START Treaty', CNN, 16 November
2010, http://politicalticker.blogs.
cnn.com/2010/11/16/cnn-poll-three-
quarters-say-ratify-start-treaty/.
This poll was consistent with others.
See http://www.rethinkmedia.org/
public-opinion/arms-control?q=
taxonomy%2Fterm%2F402 for a
summary.

9 For polling data on the Limited Test
Ban Treaty and the Intermediate
Nuclear Forces Treaty (which both

commanded broad public support) and SALT II (which produced more mixed polls) see Michael Krepon and Dan Caldwell (eds), *The Politics of Arms Control Treaty Ratification* (New York: St Martin's Press, 1991).

10 START II was ratified in 1996 (during the Clinton administration) but it did not enter into force because Russia ratified a different version. In 1999, the Senate rejected ratification of the Comprehensive Test Ban Treaty. In 1980, following the Soviet invasion of Afghanistan, President Jimmy Carter requested that the Senate delay ratification of SALT II.

11 Nolan, *An Elusive Consensus*, chapter 3.

12 Quoted in 'Fast START not Always Good', *The Augusta Chronicle*, 23 December 2010, http://chronicle.augusta.com/opinion/editorials/2010-12-23/fast-start-not-always-good?v=1293056566.

13 International Commission on Nuclear Non-proliferation and Disarmament, *Eliminating Nuclear Threats*, pp. 76–77.

Appendix

1 Norris and Kristensen, 'Global Nuclear Weapons Inventories, 1945–2010'.

2 *Ibid.*

3 'Fact Sheet: Increasing Transparency in the U.S. Nuclear Weapons Stockpile'.

4 Norris and Kristensen, 'Russian Nuclear Forces, 2010', p. 76.

5 For instance, the ranges of the *Tomahawk* Land Attack Missile/Nuclear (an American sea-launched cruise missile which is currently being retired), the Air-Launched Cruise Missile and *Polaris* A1 (the first sea-launched ballistic missile) are about 2,500km, 2,400km and 1,900km respectively. The *Tomahawk* Land Attack Missile/Nuclear and the Air-Launched Cruise Missile are equipped with different variants of the W80 warhead with reportedly identical yields. Norris and Kristensen, 'U.S. Nuclear Forces, 2006', *Bulletin of the Atomic Scientists*, vol. 62, no. 1, January/February 2006, pp. 69 and 71; Duncan Lennox (ed.), *Jane's Strategic Weapon Systems*, 39th edition, (Coulsdon: Jane's Information Group, 2003), p. 227; 'Polaris A1', Federation of American Scientists, 30 May 1997, http://www.fas.org/nuke/guide/usa/slbm/a-1.htm.

6 'Table of US Strategic Offensive Force Loadings', Natural Resources Defense Council, 25 November 2002, http://www.nrdc.org/nuclear/nudb/datab1.asp; 'Table of USSR/Russian Strategic Offensive Force Loadings', Natural Resources Defense Council, 25 November 2002, http://www.nrdc.org/nuclear/nudb/datab2.asp.

7 Norris and Kristensen, 'U.S. Nuclear Forces, 2010', p. 58; Norris and Kristensen, 'Russian Nuclear Forces, 2010', p. 74.

8 Norris and Kristensen, 'U.S. Nuclear Forces, 2009', *Bulletin of the Atomic Scientists*, vol. 65, no. 2, March–April 2009, p. 61.

9 Norris and Kristensen, 'Russian Nuclear Forces, 2010', p. 76. The SS-18, SS-19 and one variant of the SS-27 mod. 1 (usually known as Topol-M) are silo-based. All others are mobile.

10 Pavel Podvig, 'Le RS-24 est Arrivé!', Russian Strategic Nuclear Forces, 19 July 2010, http://russianforces.org/blog/2010/07/le_rs-24_est_arriv.shtml.

11 This can be inferred from Norris and Kristensen, 'U.S. Nuclear Forces, 2010'.

12 How long it would take the US to upload a significant number of warheads is unclear, although months – rather than days – appears to be the relevant timescale.

13 Oleg Bukharin, 'A Breakdown of Breakout: U.S. and Russian Warhead Production Capabilities', Arms Control Today, vol. 32, October 2002, http://www.armscontrol.org/act/2002_10/bukharinoct02.

14 Assuming the US had relatively few non-deployed strategic warheads in 1987, the size of its tactical arsenal can be estimated by subtracting the number of deployed strategic warheads (13,685) from the total size of its operational stockpile (23,575). For the relevant data see 'Fact Sheet: Increasing Transparency in the U.S. Nuclear Weapons Stockpile' and 'Table of US Strategic Offensive Force Loadings'. Russian sources place the number of Soviet tactical nuclear weapons in 1991 at about 22,000. Over the preceding few years about 2,000 weapons had been destroyed pursuant to the 1987 Intermediate Nuclear Forces Treaty. Alexander Pikayev, 'Nonstrategic Nuclear Weapons', in Arbatov and Dvorkin (eds), Nuclear Proliferation: New Technologies, Weapons, Treaties, p. 120.

15 Norris and Kristensen, 'U.S. Nuclear Forces, 2010', p. 67.

16 Norris and Kristensen, 'Russian Nuclear Forces, 2010', p. 79. For a Russian accounting see Pikayev, 'Nonstrategic Nuclear Weapons'.

Adelphi books are published eight times a year by Routledge Journals, an imprint of Taylor & Francis, 4 Park Square, Milton Park, Abingdon, Oxfordshire OX14 4RN, UK.

A subscription to the institution print edition, ISSN 0567-932X, includes free access for any number of concurrent users across a local area network to the online edition, ISSN 1478-5145.

2011 Annual Adelphi Subscription Rates			
Institution	£491	$864 USD	€726
Individual	£230	$391 USD	€312
Online only	£442	$778 USD	€653

Dollar rates apply to subscribers outside Europe. Euro rates apply to all subscribers in Europe except the UK and the Republic of Ireland where the pound sterling price applies. All subscriptions are payable in advance and all rates include postage. Journals are sent by air to the USA, Canada, Mexico, India, Japan and Australasia. Subscriptions are entered on an annual basis, i.e. January to December. Payment may be made by sterling cheque, dollar cheque, international money order, National Giro, or credit card (Amex, Visa, Mastercard).

For more information, visit our website: **http://www.informaworld.com/ adelphipapers.**

For a complete and up-to-date guide to Taylor & Francis journals and books publishing programmes, and details of advertising in our journals, visit our website: **http://www.informaworld.com.**

Ordering information:
USA/Canada: Taylor & Francis Inc., Journals Department, 325 Chestnut Street, 8th Floor, Philadelphia, PA 19106, USA. **UK/Europe/Rest of World:** Routledge Journals, T&F Customer Services, T&F Informa UK Ltd., Sheepen Place, Colchester, Essex, CO3 3LP, UK.

Advertising enquiries to:
USA/Canada: The Advertising Manager, Taylor & Francis Inc., 325 Chestnut Street, 8th Floor, Philadelphia, PA 19106, USA. Tel: +1 (800) 354 1420. Fax: +1 (215) 625 2940.

UK/Europe/Rest of World: The Advertising Manager, Routledge Journals, Taylor & Francis, 4 Park Square, Milton Park, Abingdon, Oxfordshire OX14 4RN, UK. Tel: +44 (0) 20 7017 6000. Fax: +44 (0) 20 7017 6336.

The print edition of this journal is printed on ANSI conforming acid-free paper by Bell & Bain, Glasgow, UK.